FINAL WORDS
FROM THE CROSS

Adam Hamilton

Final Words

from the Cross

ABINGDON PRESS
Nashville

FINAL WORDS FROM THE CROSS
Adam Hamilton

Copyright © 2011 by Abingdon Press

Scripture quotations, unless otherwise indicated, are from the New Revised Standard Version of the Bible, copyright © 1989 by the Division of Christian Education of the National Council of the Churches of Christ in the United States of America, and are used by permission.

Scripture quotations marked NIV are taken from the Holy Bible, NEW INTERNATIONAL VERSION®, NIV®. © 1973, 1978, 1984 by Biblica, Inc.™ Used by permission of Zondervan. All rights reserved worldwide.

Scripture quotations in this publication marked CEB are from the Common English Bible, © Copyright 2010 by Common English Bible, and are used by permission.

Scripture quotations marked ESV are from The Holy Bible, English Standard Version ®, copyright © 2001 by Crossway Bible, a publishing ministry of Good News Publishers. Used by permission. All rights reserved.

Scripture quotations marked NASB are from the New American Standard Bible®. Copyright © 1960, 1962, 1963, 1968, 1971, 1973, 1975, 1977, 1995 by The Lockman Foundation. Used by permission.

Scripture quotations marked NKJV are from the new King James Version®. Copyright © 1982 by Thomas Nelson, Inc. Used by permission. All rights reserved.

This book is printed on acid-free, elemental chlorine–free paper.

Library of Congress Cataloging-in-Publication Data

Hamilton, Adam, 1964–
    Final words from the cross / Adam Hamilton.
       p.   cm.
         ISBN 978-1-4267-4680-2 (hardback : alk. paper)   1. Jesus Christ—Seven last words—Meditations.   2. Lent—Prayers and devotions.   I. Title.
    BT457.H36   2011
    232.96'35—dc23

2011037240

11 12 13 14 15 16 17 18 19 20—10 9 8 7 6 5 4 3 2 1

MANUFACTURED IN THE UNITED STATES OF AMERICA

*I feel a great unworthiness to
comment on the dying words of Jesus.
If this book in any way helps readers to
see Jesus more clearly, to understand and
to love him more deeply, and to hear in his
dying words a word for their lives, I will be
grateful. Soli Deo Gloria.*

Contents

Contents

Introduction

In *24 Hours That Changed the World* (Abingdon, 2009) I retraced the final day of Jesus' life beginning with the Last Supper and ending with his crucifixion. In that book I devoted six chapters to the events of that final day with only a small section of one chapter focused on Jesus' final words. In this volume I'll devote six chapters to a more in-depth consideration of the six hours during which Jesus hung dying on the cross and to what are traditionally called the "seven last words" of Jesus, but which are more accurately called the seven last statements of Jesus.

When reading together the four accounts of Jesus' crucifixion, and particularly the words Jesus spoke from the cross, the reader is confronted with the fact that the Gospels do not agree as to exactly what Jesus' final words were. Matthew's and Mark's accounts have nearly word-for-word agreement. They record only one statement of Jesus from the cross—what often is called the "cry of dereliction"—in which Jesus, quoting Psalm 22:1, cries out, "My God, my God, why have you forsaken me?" Matthew and Mark both include the *ipsissima verba*—the actual words of Jesus as he spoke them in Aramaic: *"Eli, Eli, lema sabachthani?"* followed by their Greek translation. Luke and John do not record these words at all, nor do they give even a hint that Jesus felt abandoned by God. Rather, Luke and John each include three different and distinct sentences Jesus uttered from the cross, and in these words Jesus seems focused on his mission and is confident that God ultimately will deliver him.

My assumption in this book is that over the course of six hours Jesus spoke all seven of these statements recorded in the Gospels. I see them not as contradictory but as complementary. It is true that each Gospel writer's account of the final words is consistent with the way he has portrayed Jesus throughout the Gospel. Each statement tells us something important about Jesus. Together they offer a powerful and moving picture of what was on the heart and mind of Jesus as he died. It is possible that not all of the Gospel writers recalled or had access to all of these statements. It also seems likely to me that Luke and John may have been familiar with the "cry of dereliction" and that their accounts were meant to offer a counterbalance to the sense one receives from Matthew's and Mark's Gospels. Luke and John offer a kind of clarification that Jesus ultimately did not die disillusioned and feeling abandoned by God; rather, his final words and thoughts were words of complete trust in his Father.

A word about the order of the last statements of Jesus: Because no one Gospel includes more than three of the final seven phrases Jesus spoke, we do not know the exact order in which Jesus spoke these words during the six hours on the cross. I have used, in this book, the traditional ordering of these statements:

> "Father, forgive them; for they do not know what
> they are doing."
> "Today you will be with me in Paradise."
> "Behold your son. . . . Behold your mother."
> "My God, my God, why have you forsaken me?"
> "I thirst."
> "It is finished."
> "Into your hands I commit my spirit."

I have combined the final two statements of Jesus into one chapter, allowing the book to coincide with the six weeks of Lent. I also have included a postscript, "The Words After That," an Easter meditation on the words Jesus spoke following his resurrection, including what were truly the final words Jesus spoke while walking this earth.

In this book I've chosen to begin each chapter with a first-person narrative of someone who stood near the cross, hearing the particular statement of Jesus. My hope in doing so is to help you imagine yourself at the foot of the cross and to help you see and hear what transpired there. These accounts are, of course, fictional, though they are imagined based upon the information we do have from the Gospels.

It should be mentioned that in *Twenty-Four Hours That Changed the World* I prepared video segments in which I took viewers to the Holy Land to visit the traditional sites where the final events of Jesus' life are said to have occurred. Available for this present volume is a small group discussion guide and DVD with videos not filmed in the Holy Land but edited from sermons I preached on the Final Words—a series of sermons that served as the basis of this book. The videos are designed to promote discussion among book clubs, Bible study groups, and Sunday school classes.

Let us join the crowd now and experience the final words from the cross.

1.

"Father, Forgive Them . . ."

As they led him away, they seized a man, Simon of Cyrene, who was coming from the country, and they laid the cross on him, and made him carry it behind Jesus. . . . When they came to the place that is called The Skull, they crucified Jesus there with the criminals, one on his right and one on his left. Then Jesus said, "Father, forgive them; for they do not know what they are doing." (Luke 23:26, 33-34a)

Simon of Cyrene

We had spent two weeks sailing from the north coast of Africa to celebrate the Passover in Jerusalem. My sons were small boys, yet old enough to feel the excitement as we approached the Holy City. As our small caravan came over the last hill, Rufus let out a shout, "Look, Father, the Temple!" There she stood, the earthly palace of God, gleaming as she towered over the city. Though my family had lived in Cyrene for generations, Jerusalem was for us, as for every Jew, our heart's home.

That night we joined our cousins in Bethany for the Passover Seder that marked the beginning of the Festival, sharing a meal and recalling God's salvation of our people. We ended that meal, as we did every year, praying for the coming of the Messiah. The next morning Rufus, Alexander, and I left early to spend the day in Jerusalem, visiting the Temple and then the Festival taking place near the markets.

As we approached the city we saw what appeared to be a parade coming our way. But soon we could see that this was no parade. There were Roman soldiers driving three criminals toward the rock quarry where criminals were crucified. Each of these criminals was carrying a heavy beam across his shoulders. One clearly had been badly beaten, for his body was bloodied and he looked as though he could barely walk. I took Rufus and Alexander by the hand and pulled them away from the road. I did not want them to see this terrible thing.

Just then the tragic figure, the sorely wounded man, stumbled and fell at my feet. I saw that his brow was wrapped in a crude crown of thorns, and suddenly I realized who this man was. This was Jesus of Nazareth, whom some had claimed was the Messiah. He had been critical of the Jewish leadership in Jerusalem. I could not believe it—they had actually sentenced him to death.

Everything happened so quickly. I was lost in my thoughts when I heard one of the soldiers say, "You there! You carry his cross! And you, Jesus, get to your feet!" There was nothing I could do. I told my boys, "Stay close." I picked up the beam, far heavier than I had imagined, and pitched it over my shoulder. Then I reached out a hand to Jesus to help him up. He was clearly in pain. But there was still, in his face, a strength and determination. He looked me in the eyes, as if to thank me, and then he set his face toward Calvary.

It was only a five-minute walk to the place they called The Skull—Calvary—where the Romans crucified their victims. Dropping the beam before the executioners, I stepped back, searching for my boys. And then we stood and watched as they assembled the cross. Then they stripped Jesus naked and laid him atop the beams. They stretched his arms to the sides before they drove the spikes into his wrists as he shouted in pain. Then they nailed his ankles into the side of the cross, one on the right and one on the left. Finally, they hoisted his cross up and in position and, as they did, he let out another shout of pain.

Because I had never been so close to a crucifixion, I had not realized what a horrible thing this was. Rufus began to cry. Alexander became nauseous. There were two thieves being crucified with Jesus, and the soldiers hoisted each one into the air.

The Romans shouted to the crowd, "Take a look at your king now! This is a lesson from Rome—don't forget it!" The soldiers, laughing, began to throw dice for his clothing. Some in the crowd wept. Others hurled insults at him. The religious leaders stood with their arms crossed, a strange expression of satisfaction upon their faces.

And then Jesus took a deep breath, and someone in the crowd said, "Shh! He's about to say something." This is what he said: "Father, forgive them; for they do not know what they are doing."

I would never forget these words. A dying man, tortured and crucified, praying that God would forgive his tormentors. What kind of man would do such a thing? His words would haunt me the rest of my life. Ultimately, they would be the reason I became one of his followers.

I have been with dozens of people as they were approaching death. A person's dying words sometimes simply express his or her needs: "Could you please move the pillow?" or "May I have a drink?" Sometimes they express a concern for others—a final "I love you" or "It's going to be okay." A person's final words reveal what is on his or her heart at the time, and sometimes they reveal the nature of the person's faith and hope. John Wesley is said to have uttered these words as he died: "Best of all, God is with us."

In the case of one being crucified, the very act of speaking was painful and required great exertion. It is thought that death comes to those being crucified due to some combination of exhaustion, shock, buildup of fluid around the heart and in the lungs, and asphyxiation. To speak while being crucified would require great effort as the victim would have to pull himself up by the nails in the wrists in order to expand the diaphragm to speak. For all of these reasons, words were sparse among the victims of crucifixion.

The Gospels record seven statements Jesus made from the cross. There are three reasons why we can assume these statements are important and should be considered for what they teach us about Jesus, about his Father, and about ourselves. First, Jesus went to some effort and bore great pain to speak them. Second, Jesus came to reveal God—to be God's "word made flesh." And finally, the Gospel writers, as they were trying to communicate not only who Jesus was and what he did but also the significance of his life, felt it important to include his dying words.

We begin our study of Jesus' final words with the first words from the cross recorded by Luke, words uttered by Jesus just after he was crucified: "Father, forgive them; for they do not know what they are doing" (23:34).

Let's start with a word about how this beautiful statement may have come to be included in Luke's Gospel. If you read the footnote in your Bible related to these words from the cross, you will discover that they were likely not included in the earliest editions of the Gospel of Luke. Because Luke was, in some ways, a historian who wrote his Gospel account by interviewing the people who knew Jesus personally, it is likely that the people he interviewed did not know that Jesus made this comment from the cross. This would explain why Luke omitted them; he recorded only those statements that the persons he interviewed knew Jesus had made.

As Luke's Gospel began to be copied and shared in churches around the Roman Empire, it came to a city where someone who had been an eyewitness at the cross actually lived. That eyewitness remembered something Jesus had said from the cross that forever changed his life. Upon reading the Gospel he said, "There was something else. He said something else—something too important to leave out." And because this eyewitness was known by all to have been at the cross, it was felt appropriate to add to Luke's words this phrase, "Father, forgive them; for they do not know what they are doing."

One suggestion for this eyewitness at the cross is Rufus. In Mark 15:21 we learn that Simon of Cyrene carried Jesus' cross, and that he had two sons, Alexander and Rufus. Mark is thought to have written his Gospel in Rome, the earliest of the Gospels. His mention of Alexander and Rufus seems strange unless Alexander and Rufus were boys who grew up to be known leaders in the church. In Romans 16:13, Paul writes,

"Greet Rufus, chosen in the Lord; and greet his mother—a mother to me also." It seems likely to some that this is the same Rufus, now a leader in Rome, who stood by and watched Jesus crucified when he was a boy. Hence, it is suggested that the phrase "Father forgive them; for they do not know what they are doing" was added as a result of the authority and testimony of Rufus.

I mention this only as a suggestion for how our present statement came to be in the Gospels. Scholars have a host of other suggestions, but it seems to me that something like this points toward what may have happened and why this statement, though not in Luke's earliest editions, is an authentic statement of Jesus from the cross.

With this as an introduction, let's consider the significance of these words.

"Father, Forgive *Them*"

It is not surprising that these words—the first words spoken by Jesus from the cross—were a prayer. What is surprising, haunting, and, for some, disturbing, is what he prayed: "Father, forgive them; for they do not know what they are doing." Let's begin our exploration of this prayer with a question: For whom was Jesus praying? Who was the "them" Jesus was asking God to forgive?

He was, of course, praying for the soldiers who cruelly tortured him and crucified him and who were preparing to gamble for his clothes. "Father, forgive *them*."

He also was praying for the crowd who, even now, were beginning their verbal assault on him—Luke notes that they were deriding him, shaking their heads and mocking him. For them he prayed, "Father, forgive *them*."

Then there were the religious leaders who, from their own jealousy and spiritual blindness, conspired with the Romans to kill him, just as the false prophets of Jeremiah's day had sought to kill him. For these hypocritical leaders he prayed, "Father, forgive *them*."

This is astounding! Can you imagine such mercy? That Jesus would pray for *them* as he hung on the cross is one of the most powerful images in all the Gospels.

But there is someone else included in Jesus' prayer, someone for whom Jesus was pleading from the cross for God's mercy to be extended: *We* are among the "them" Jesus was praying for as he said, "Father, forgive *them*; for they do not know what they are doing."

There's an old gospel hymn that asks, "Were you there when they crucified my Lord?" The answer is that, in a profound spiritual sense, you *were* there. The entire human race was there at the Crucifixion. The death of Jesus was an event that transcended time. Jesus' prayer gave voice to what Jesus was doing on the cross. He was offering himself to God his Father as an offering of atonement. In this moment he was both the High Priest pleading for atonement for the human race and the offering itself. This sacrificial act

19

was for those who had come before and for those who would come after just as much as it was for those who heard his words that day.

You and I *were* there when they crucified the Lord. In a sense, Jesus prayed, "Father, forgive Adam. Forgive (*insert your name*). Forgive those in our churches and those on the streets. Forgive those in the suburbs and those downtown. Forgive those in our country and those on the other side of the world. Father, forgive *them*. . . ." This is the power of the words Jesus cried out from the cross: They were prayed not only for those who stood by at the cross, but also for all of us—for all of humanity.

With that in mind, let us consider three additional truths that these words of Jesus teach us.

We Need Forgiveness

The fact that Jesus devoted one of his seven last statements to a prayer for our forgiveness tells us something significant: we *need* forgiveness. It wasn't just those around the cross who needed forgiveness; we need forgiveness, too. Our need for forgiveness and God's willingness to give it are two of the major themes of the Bible. We need forgiveness because we struggle with sin. *Sin* is a word that many of us prefer not to use today. We'd prefer "mistake" or "slip up." The Greek and Hebrew words most often translated as "sin" in the Bible are words that mean "to stray from the path" or "to miss the mark." The implication is that God has a path or way that we were intended to live, but we don't follow that path. Instead we all stray from it.

The church traditionally lists seven deadly sins as the root of all other sins. You may remember the traditional list: lust, gluttony, greed, sloth, wrath, envy, and pride. When I pursue these impulses, I step away from God's path and depart from God's will. These paths promise pleasure and happiness, but they ultimately lead to pain. They dehumanize us and others and separate us from God by means of guilt and shame; they hurt others and keep us from doing the things that God intends and from being the people God intends.

I am reminded of a man who came into my office having been involved in an extramarital affair. He had learned that the person he had been intimate with had a sexually transmitted disease, which he had in turn passed on to his wife. His wife wanted a divorce. He was losing the thing that he loved most in life—his family. He wept as he described the guilt, shame, and sense of despair he felt. He was not thinking of any of these things the night he gave into the temptation to sleep with a woman he'd just met while on a business trip. The path that promised pleasure and joy led to heartache and pain.

On a global scale, *sin* is perhaps the best word to describe the quest for power, the genocide, the cruelty and inhumanity, and the bigotry and hate that is behind so much human suffering and war in our world today.

Some suggest that Christians spend too much time dwelling on sin and making people feel guilty. Some Christians and churches may do that, but that is not the central focus of the gospel. The central focus of the gospel is grace and God's mercy. Still, you cannot appreciate God's mercy until you know you need it. And we all need it. We all struggle with doing the wrong thing. Something inside us lures us to do the things that are not God's will. When theologians speak of "original sin" they typically are referring to the impulse of the human heart that makes sin captivating and alluring. There is debate about what is meant by *original*. Traditionally this word has been understood to mean that sin was passed down from Adam and Eve. However we acquired it, we all are affected and, in a sense, infected by it. The desire for what will hurt us and separate us from God is a part of the human condition. This tendency starts at an early age.

As I was reflecting upon these words of Jesus from the cross, I was reminded of something I did when I was eight or nine years old. One day I walked to a nearby shopping center. There was a department store that sold, among other things, record albums. I went to look at the albums by the Beatles. I had been saving a bit of money to buy one, but I discovered that I was two dollars short. Then an idea came into my eight-year-old brain. Some of the records were on sale, and some were not. I thought, *My record should be on sale.* So I peeled off a sale sticker from a record that was on sale, and I placed it on the Beatles album I wanted that was not on sale. Inside I knew it was wrong. I took it to the register; my heart was pounding out of my chest at the thought that someone would figure out what I had done. Today, with the scanners that are used to identify the item and price, swapping tags like that would never work. You would be caught. But I wasn't caught, and I walked away, essentially stealing from the store.

I was only eight, and I was a thief. I never did that again, but I did many other things when I was growing up that I'm not proud of. Unfortunately, as we become adults, we don't stop sinning. Our sins merely become more sophisticated, and we become more adept at justifying them. Sin is a problem we never outgrow.

So, when Christianity speaks of sin, the aim is not to make us feel guilty but to help us discover the grace and healing mercy of God that we so desperately need.

When Christianity speaks of sin, the aim is not to make us feel guilty but to help us discover the grace and healing mercy of God that we so desperately need.

Imagine you've been having chest pains and shortness of breath, and now you're experiencing pain in your arm. Although you might say, "It's really nothing; I'm not going to worry about it," it's possible you're having a heart attack and need to be examined by a doctor. If you leave this unchecked, you could die an early death. If you are wise, you will want to know what's causing these symptoms and will go to the doctor. If the doctor says, "Listen, we've found serious blockage, and you need surgery," would you think that the doctor is being overly pessimistic or trying to help you so that you can get better? Would you say, "That doctor is such a downer! I don't want to hear that. I'm going to find a doctor who will make me feel good about my heart"? Of course not! You would be thankful that the doctor found the problem and could cure it with surgery.

In a similar way, the gospel's focus is not on sin; sin is simply the diagnosis. The gospel's focus is on the cure, which is God's grace and gift of salvation. It is heart surgery conducted by the divine physician who laid down his life for us.

This is what the season of Lent is all about—the forty-day season in which we examine our hearts and minds and lives to see why we need what Jesus prayed for and died for: our forgiveness. This leads us to another truth that this prayer of Jesus teaches us.

God's Grace Is a Gift

Jesus was not merely pointing out sin; he was praying for God's mercy toward those who sin. What makes this prayer of Jesus remarkable is that he prayed for God's mercy for those who stood at the foot of the cross while they were still tormenting him. They were spitting on him and hurling insults at him and gambling for his clothes when he prayed, "Father, forgive them." Jesus prayed for them and for us before any of us realized our need—and while we were still in the midst of our sin. The apostle Paul captures it this way in Romans 5:6-8:

For while we were still weak, at the right time Christ died for the ungodly. Indeed, rarely will anyone die for a righteous person—though perhaps for a good person someone might actually dare to die. But God proves his love for us in that while we still were sinners Christ died for us.

This idea that Jesus was praying from the cross for our forgiveness, and that he was, even before we repented, dying for us, is a mind-bending idea. Before you were born, God knew the sinful things you would do and forgave you in advance. On the cross Jesus suffered and died to save you from your sins and redeem you.

Let me pause to answer an important question people often ask: *How does Jesus' death on the cross save me from my sins?* There are different ways of understanding our redemption—different theories of the Atonement—but let me offer one example from a dramatic act in the Old Testament that illustrates the spiritual truth of atonement.

God commanded Moses to atone for the people's sins every year by bringing two goats before the Lord. One would be slaughtered, the other sent away into the wilderness (see Leviticus 16). The priest would cast lots for which goat would be sacrificed and which would be sent to the wilderness. The one that was sacrificed was brought before God, the sins of the people were symbolically laid upon it, and it was butchered and burned. This goat would be an offering on behalf of the people—a kind of visual apology and sign of their repentance. The priest would then place his hands on the head of the second goat, the "scapegoat," and pronounce the sins of the people on the head of the goat. Then they would drive the goat out into the wilderness never to be seen again—presumably to be eaten by some wild animal or to live out its days in the wilderness. The visual image was that the people's sins were carried away; their sins went with the goat.

Could a goat really bear sins and carry them away into the wilderness and thus procure forgiveness and atonement? Of course not. The scapegoat, as well as the animal that was slaughtered, were merely outward ways of communicating deeper spiritual truths. God wanted the Israelites to understand that sin is deadly, and that grace is not cheap. God wanted to give them a tangible means by which they could express their remorse and by which God could express divine grace. I believe God wanted them to feel the weight of sin. At the same time, in the scapegoat God wanted them to see and know that their sins were truly forgiven. God took something tangible to reveal something intangible yet profoundly true. The slaughtered goat and the scapegoat were part of a divine drama meant to reveal the deadliness of sin and the costliness of grace.

In a similar way, one of the things we understand about Jesus' death on the cross is that it is a divine drama. John tells us that Jesus was God's "word" made flesh. He was both God's messenger and God's message. Every part of his life was God's word, God's self-revelation to God's people. On the cross, the sins of the world—all the hatred, unfaithfulness, bigotry, poverty, violence, and death—were placed upon the "Lamb of God who takes away the sins of the world." When we see Jesus hanging there on the cross we are meant to see the costliness of grace. Our sin is not a trifling thing. The Son of God was crucified for it. Yet we are also meant to see on the cross God's willingness to extend mercy and grace. As we look back on the cross two thousand years later, we understand that God's gift of forgiveness and mercy is an accomplished feat. It has been completed in the past, but for each of us it only becomes real as we accept it in the present.

A few years ago we were taking our Christmas tree down ten days after Christmas, and a gift fell out of the tree—it had been placed up in the tree by the one who had given it to us but we didn't realize it was in there. We had had that gift for a month, but we had not unwrapped it or been able to enjoy using it.

This is how it is with God's mercy. God has already done everything necessary to save us and to forgive us. We don't earn our salvation: it is pure gift. We are saved by God's grace—saved from ourselves and from our sin. We have been reconciled to God. God, through Jesus, has already forgiven us. Our task is to accept the gift.

Even our ability to understand and accept the gift is by God's grace—by God's work in our lives to draw us to God.

John Wesley spoke of this as God's *prevenient* grace. *Prevenient* is a word that means "that which goes before." This prevenient grace is God's mercy that is extended to us and begins to work in us even before we turn to God and repent, preparing us to understand our need for God's mercy and to help us accept the gift of God's salvation.

On many occasions I have spoken with men and women who were overcome by their own sin and guilt. One day I was talking in my office with a man who was weeping over things he'd done to hurt others in the past and the pain he felt—the separation from God and from those he'd hurt. Of course, he needed to seek forgiveness and make amends with those whom he had wronged. But the first step he needed to take was to ask for God's forgiveness. We went into the sanctuary and walked to the cross. I said, "Look at the cross. It was there that Christ purchased your forgiveness. It was there he prayed, 'Father, forgive them; for they do not know what they are doing.' He prayed that for you. He has already prayed for your forgiveness." We stood there in front of the cross and prayed together. With tears coming down his cheeks, he finally understood that God's grace was a very costly gift, but that it was already paid for, awaiting his acceptance of it.

On another occasion, a young man in our congregation who had gone off to college and had really made a mess of his life with drugs and alcohol returned home from college on Christmas break. After nearly dying in an automobile accident he came to his senses. One day he came into the sanctuary when no one else was there, and he walked up to the cross above our choir loft. He wrapped his arms around it and began to cry. He knew intuitively that what was necessary for his forgiveness and salvation had already been given. He just needed to claim it.

God knows the things we've done of which we're embarrassed or ashamed. God knows our humanity and how easily we get off course. And knowing all of that—all we have ever done, and all we will ever do—Jesus prayed, "Father, forgive them."

Never have human beings done anything so dark as to condemn, torture, and then crucify the Son of God, and yet Jesus prayed for them even as they were in the midst of their sin, asking that they might receive mercy. If mercy was available to them—and it was—then I promise you it is available to you. The gift of salvation has already been given to you. Your task is to receive it, to trust it, and to walk in the joy of your forgiveness and salvation.

Jesus Modeled Forgiveness

God's grace is not only a gift; it also is an example for us. Jesus could have prayed this prayer in silence, but he chose to pray it aloud. He wanted us to "overhear" this prayer. He not only wanted us to know we're forgiven; he wanted to teach us what it means to be his follower. Those of us who choose to follow Jesus must practice forgiveness, just as he did.

Jesus lived the only perfect life, and he showed us what it means to be authentically human. He walked God's path, offering mercy and grace, and he said, "Come, follow me." So, when we become his followers, we are to move away from the path on which we do things that hurt ourselves and others and separate us from God, and we are to begin following Jesus on the path he intends us to walk—a path marked by grace and mercy and forgiveness.

Jesus spent much of his ministry teaching about the importance of forgiving others. In the Sermon on the Mount, he taught, "Blessed are the merciful, for they will receive mercy" (Matthew 5:7). Then he taught his disciples to "love your enemies and pray for those who persecute you" (Matthew 5:44). When the disciples asked how they should pray, Jesus told them to pray, "Forgive us for the ways we have wronged you, just as we also forgive those who have wronged us" (Matthew 6:12 CEB). He also taught them, "If you forgive others their sins, your heavenly Father will also forgive you" (Matthew 6:14 CEB).

That's a perplexing verse. Does that mean that God will not forgive us if we do not forgive other people? Well, not exactly. Remember, God has already forgiven us. The question is whether we will accept the gift of forgiveness that God has offered. If you are someone who resents other people and refuses to forgive them, then you carry bitterness in your heart toward them. That makes it very hard for you to accept God's forgiveness, because in your heart you are unwilling to forgive others. How can you truly know God's mercy when you are unwilling to extend mercy? Because you do not forgive, you assume that God is like you. Because you carry resentment for a long time, you may subconsciously believe that God must be the same way. People who regularly forgive others, on the other hand, find it easier to believe and trust in the grace of God because their hearts have been enlarged by grace, and they freely offer it to others.

People who regularly forgive others . . . find it easier . . . to believe and trust in the grace of God because their hearts have been enlarged by grace, and they freely offer it to others.

It's one thing to teach about forgiveness; it's another to model it. On the cross, Jesus actually modeled forgiveness in the most difficult of circumstances. He spoke this prayer out loud to show us how to forgive. Jesus was saying, "This is what forgiveness looks like."

Forgiveness is the answer to so much of the pain in this world. The war between combatants is about getting even, but forgiveness is about getting along. It's the key to relationships. A marriage won't survive more than a year without one or both spouses saying from time to time, "I am sorry" and "I forgive you." Marriage simply cannot succeed without grace and forgiveness. Likewise, you cannot have a friendship over the long term apart from forgiveness.

It holds true in every area of life. If you hold grudges in business, you're going to be the most miserable person to work around. If you refuse to forgive friends and neighbors, you're going to find yourself isolated and lonely.

Yet forgiveness is hard for us. It is hard because there is something inside of us that wants justice for those who've wronged us, even as we desire mercy for ourselves. The beauty of mercy and the hypocrisy of our seeking justice for those who wrong us while seeking mercy for ourselves are captured so powerfully in the courtroom scene in Shakespeare's *Merchant of Venice,* where Portia is pleading for Shylock to offer mercy to Antonio rather than to seek justice.

> The quality of mercy is not strain'd,
> It droppeth as the gentle rain from heaven
> Upon the place beneath: it is twice blest;
> It blesseth him that gives and him that takes:
> 'Tis mightiest in the mightiest: it becomes

The throned monarch better than his crown;
His sceptre shows the force of temporal power,
The attribute to awe and majesty,
Wherein doth sit the dread and fear of kings;
But mercy is above this sceptred sway;
It is enthroned in the hearts of kings,
It is an attribute to God himself;
And earthly power doth then show likest God's
        When mercy seasons justice.

Having described the quality of mercy and its desirability, Portia comes back to the topic of justice saying,

Though justice be thy plea, consider this,
That, in the course of justice, none of us
Should see salvation: we do pray for mercy;
And that same prayer doth teach us all to render
        The deeds of mercy.
                                        (*Merchant of Venice*, Act 4, Scene 1)

Like us, and like old Shylock, the disciples apparently struggled with forgiveness. They asked Jesus, "How often must we forgive? Is seven times enough?" Jesus responded, "Not seven times, but seventy-seven times" (Matthew 18:21-22 NIV). In essence, we are to keep forgiving.

What's more, we are to forgive without reservation. Jesus once told a parable about a father who forgave his wayward son *before* the son could speak a word of repentance. That doesn't mean there are no consequences. We can forgive others, and love them, yet not want to be around them very much anymore. There are legal consequences, and sometimes there are financial consequences. Even so, forgiveness can flow.

Forgiveness is a complicated issue at times. There are people whose salvation is actually harmed when we extend forgiveness to them before they have repented. But there are other situations when the extending of mercy before someone asks actually leads the other to repentance. Some people will never repent or ask for our forgiveness. But in these cases, we still must learn the art of forgiving. The alternative is to be consumed by resentment, anger, and hate.

As often as I've preached on forgiveness, I still find there are moments when a resentment I thought I had let go of comes back to me and I feel the anger creeping back into my heart. The prayer of Jesus on the cross is meant to become our prayer. If Jesus can pray, "Father, forgive them; for they do not know what they are doing," then with his help, I can, too.

I found myself wrestling with feelings of resentment just recently as I was thinking of something someone said to me last year. Though I have forgiven the person and have let it go a dozen times, the resentment crept back into my thinking once more. Somehow, looking at the cross and hearing Jesus pray this prayer as the soldiers, merchants, and religious leaders stood by, continuing to inflict their pain, led me to want to be like him and pray, "Father, forgive them; for they do not know what they are doing." As I did, I found the freedom that comes from releasing resentment and bitterness and replacing it with grace.

Existentialist theologian Paul Tillich, writing in a sermon entitled "To Whom Much Is Forgiven . . ." notes, "Forgiveness is an answer, the divine answer, to the question implied in our existence."[1] On the cross Jesus' first words demonstrate God's willingness to forgive our sins, and they call us to become people who follow in his path—people who can pray, "Father, forgive them; for they do not know what they are doing."

———————

Take a moment to think about people who have wronged you. Perhaps even write their names here on this page. Would you be willing now to join in the prayer that Jesus prayed for those who crucified him?

Father, forgive them. Father, you know their heart, and you know my pain. I pray for those who hurt me. Forgive them, and heal me. Amen.

2.

"Today You Will Be With Me in Paradise"

Two others also, who were criminals, were led away to be put to death with him. . . . One of the criminals who were hanged there kept deriding him and saying, "Are you not the Messiah? Save yourself and us!" But the other rebuked him, saying, "Do you not fear God, since you are under the same sentence of condemnation? And we indeed have been condemned justly, for we are getting what we deserve for our deeds, but this man has done nothing wrong." Then he said, "Jesus, remember me when you come into your kingdom." He replied, "Truly I tell you, today you will be with me in Paradise." (Luke 23:32, 39-43)

The Thief on the Cross

He looked at me with compassion.

It had been a long time since I had felt anyone's compassion. My mother died when I was seven. My father was a drunkard whose idea of encouragement was to call me an idiot and to tell me to leave him alone. So I did. I began committing petty crimes when I was ten. I'd committed armed robbery when I was fifteen. And I killed a man before I was twenty. I was a hopeless cause.

And here I was, 47 years old, carrying my cross on the way to Calvary. It was amusing to me that Jesus of Nazareth was being crucified with us. I knew of him. Some among my friends had gone to hear him. Jesus had even eaten with them. I knew some of the girls who had found religion by listening to him. They claimed he was God's Messiah.

Strange Messiah—befriending sinners and prostitutes. If I believed in God, that's the kind of Messiah I would want. But I didn't, and so I was sure he wasn't.

Yet I can tell you this: I could not take my eyes off of him.

A huge crowd came out for his crucifixion—the money-changers, the religious leaders, the Romans, and all those religious hypocrites. They stood around him, hurling insults at him. I joined in at first, glad they weren't insulting me. But even I didn't have the stomach for it. It was then I heard him praying from his cross, "Father, forgive them; for they do not know what they are doing." I was stunned—this friend of sinners prayed for mercy for his enemies.

He turned and looked at me as if he could see right through me; once more he looked at me with compassion. Even in my pain, I found myself drawn to this man. If, as some said, he was sent from God, and if God was like this man, showing mercy to sinners, then perhaps there was hope for me. Levi, my partner in crime, began to hurl insults at Jesus once more. I shouted, "Levi, stop it! Don't you see? We're getting what we deserve. He's done nothing wrong." And then, for reasons I still don't understand, I turned to Jesus and said, "Jesus, remember me when you come into your kingdom." He replied, "Truly I tell you, today you will be with me in Paradise."

Luke is my favorite among the Gospels. His Gospel highlights Jesus' concern for the least, the last and the lost. The Gospel begins by highlighting Jesus' lowly position— born in a stable with a feeding trough for a crib. In Luke's description of Jesus' ministry, we find Jesus consistently concerned for the sinner, the outcast, the unclean, and the nobody. In the Gospel of Luke, Jesus clearly identifies his mission as coming to "seek out and to save the lost" (Luke 19:10). It is not surprising, then, that only Luke's Gospel records a conversation Jesus has as he hangs dying beside a thief. As we consider this conversation, we'll focus on the words of Jesus and ask: What does this scene teach us about Jesus, and what does it teach us about ourselves?

Jesus Associated With Sinners

It is said that a person is known by the company he or she keeps. In life and in death, Jesus associated with sinners. This troubled the religious people. In Luke 15:1-2 we read, "Now all the tax collectors and sinners were coming near to listen to him. And the Pharisees and the scribes were grumbling and saying, 'This fellow welcomes sinners and eats with them.' "

Jesus allowed the prostitute to wash his feet with her tears. He called tax collectors and garden-variety sinners to be his disciples. He touched lepers and ate with unclean people.

We see this kind of association throughout his ministry. In Jesus' day, nonreligious people generally did not like associating with religious people. They likely felt they had to watch their language and pretend to be something they weren't because they did not want to feel the judgment and scorn of the religious people.

It is still that way for many nonreligious and nominally religious people today. They might think about going to church, but then they think about what it feels like when they walk into church—and it doesn't feel good. The preacher seems to talk down to people like them, making them feel small.

But when Jesus was around nonreligious people, they didn't feel small. They didn't feel like nobodies. They didn't feel like sinners. They just felt like people who came to hear the good news of God in a way that made sense to them, and they found that they wanted to know more about this God Jesus talked about.

Jesus gave his personal mission statement just days before he was crucified. He had gone into the town of Jericho and made his way to a large sycamore tree in the center of the city. Sitting in the branches of that tree was one of the town's most notorious sinners. His name was Zacchaeus. Zacchaeus had attempted to catch a glimpse of Jesus as he entered Jericho, but the town's folk were not fond of Zacchaeus. He had sold his soul to the Romans, buying the right to collect taxes for Rome—a position that allowed him to get rich at the expense of the people. That's why they were not about to let him through to catch a glimpse of Jesus. So Zacchaeus shimmied up the large sycamore tree in the center of town. There he sat, looking at Jesus. Jesus made his way straight for that tree and said, "Zacchaeus, come down from there. I want to stay at your house today" (See Luke 19:5).

Eating supper with someone in the Middle East in biblical times meant you were willing to call that person your friend. So when Jesus said that he wanted to stay with Zacchaeus, and later ate with him, the religious people couldn't believe it. Why would Jesus stay with a known reprobate like Zacchaeus?

Zacchaeus invited all his sinful friends for supper that night—prostitutes, tax collectors, and thieves. I picture Jesus eating with them, laughing and telling stories about the kingdom of God in a way that made the people want to know more. And I picture the religious people standing outside, waving their fingers and saying, "Why does he eat with people like that?" That's when I imagine Jesus got up from the table, went to the religious people, and said, "You just don't understand, do you?" And then he gave them his personal life mission statement: "The Son of Man came to seek out and to save the lost" (Luke 19:10).

As Jesus lived, so he died. Even as he was crucified, Jesus was carrying out his mission statement and associating with sinners. Jesus did not die alone. His companions at Calvary were two criminals. Three times Luke described them with the Greek word *kakourgoi*, which literally means "those who do evil works." Matthew and Mark described them as *lestai*, a term that is used of armed robbers. In Jesus' parable of the good Samaritan, it was a band of *lestai* that accosted a certain man as he was going from Jerusalem to Jericho. They stripped him, beat him, and left him half dead. *Lestai* are the kind of criminals who would use violence to take what they wanted, leaving a man in the Judean desert to die at the side of the road.

The scene of Jesus and the two *lestai* is among the most powerful in all the Bible. Jesus, the only fully righteous and sinless human being—he who spelled out his mission by saying, "The Son of Man came to seek out and to save the lost" (Luke 19:10)—had his final conversation with a criminal and thug who was rethinking life in response to Jesus' character and mercy; and Jesus offered the man eternal life.

Do you see how important reaching lost people was—and is—to Jesus? It was what drove him to the cross, so that in his dying he might save the human race from self-destruction, self-worship, and sin; and so that in his resurrection he might save us from death.

If this is what mattered most to Jesus—reaching people who were lost—what does that mean for us as his followers? If Jesus wasn't afraid to associate with criminals, prostitutes, and people who were considered unclean, what is the application for us?

Let's make it even more personal. Do people who do not know Jesus Christ feel comfortable around you? Do they feel small or valued and accepted after they have had a conversation with you? Are you willing to associate with people others might consider riffraff, and would you show them kindness and compassion because that's what it means to be a follower of Jesus? Do they feel comfortable in your church?

One of the ministries at The United Methodist Church of the Resurrection that exemplifies this mission of Jesus is our prison ministry. We have a team of people

Are you willing to associate with people others might consider riffraff, and would you show them kindness and compassion because that's what it means to be a follower of Jesus?

who go to the prisons and minister with men and women who are incarcerated. Ron is one of the volunteers who works in our ministry at Leavenworth Penitentiary.

Ron was in law enforcement for twenty years, and after he retired, people at our church began to say, "Ron, why don't you join the prison ministry?" Ron's response was something along these lines: "You're kidding, right? I mean, I put those people there. You think I want to go visit them? You want me to share Christ with them? I know what they're like. I'm not going there." But God is persistent; the Holy Spirit kept nudging him, and people kept asking. So, finally, Ron began working in the prison ministry. And something happened: God filled Ron's heart with compassion for the men he visited. Though he knew what they were like and even had helped put some of them there, Ron began to reach out and to love them. And as he showed them compassion, kindness, gentleness, and love, they were drawn to him. These young guys began to look at him as a father figure, a father they never had.

I asked Ron to tell me about some of the men he has visited whose lives have changed, and he told me about a guy we will call Mike. When Mike was a little boy, he was physically abused by his stepfather. At one point, Mike actually was thrown through the kitchen window by his stepfather. Over time he hardened his heart to protect himself from being hurt by others. Eventually, he began to stay away from home as much as possible. By the time he was fourteen, he moved out on his own. That's when he began to get into trouble.

At first it was petty theft, and then he stole his first car at the age of sixteen. He discovered he had two options: go to jail or join the army. He had already been kicked out of high school, so his parents signed a waiver for him to join the army. At age seventeen, he was able to be fully deployed. That's when he stole his second car—a brand-new Nissan 300z. He drove it across four states in a high-speed chase. He was arrested and thrown in jail for a couple of years.

When Mike got out of prison, he decided he would switch from stealing cars to robbing banks. In his first 120 days as a bank robber, he hit more than a dozen banks. There were sixteen federal charges filed against him in four different states. He was arrested, put in jail, and tried; and he was found to be a hopeless cause. They gave him twenty years in prison.

While he was in prison this time, he tried to escape. When they caught him, they put him in maximum confinement, and he found himself in the same cell block with John Gotti, the mobster, and a whole host of other people you would not want to hang around with.

Then one day several years ago Mike woke up and realized what a mess he had made of his life. He felt like he was a hopeless cause. The question he kept asking himself was, *Where do I go for hope?* Finally, he decided that maybe Jesus might offer him hope. So one day he prayed, "Jesus, no longer my will, but your will be done. I want to follow you." The guys in our prison ministry were involved with him at this point, and God sent Ron to be his mentor.

You need to know something else. Mike had joined the Aryan brotherhood as a teenager. He was a white supremacist. Ron, our prison ministry volunteer, is African American. Ron showed such compassion and love that Mike came to see he really was not a hopeless cause after all. According to Ron, Mike is a different person today. In the words of the apostle

Paul, Mike has become a new creature in Christ. The old has passed away and the new has come. He has been born anew—born of the Spirit.

What would happen if every one of us who professes to be a Christian would reach out to those who are lost and show them love and compassion in Jesus' name? How would the world change?

Reaching those who are lost was the driving mission of Jesus, and it is meant to be our driving mission as his followers. Jesus died for those who are sinners, and even in his dying he was reaching out to people whom others considered hopeless causes.

Two Criminals, Two Responses

Another thing we can see in this scene, as we look at the two criminals crucified on either side of Jesus, is two possible responses we might make to Jesus. Both criminals saw the same thing that day: a man who claimed to be the Messiah—the revolutionary king—abused and crucified. They saw all the cruelty and hate heaped upon Jesus by the crowd. They heard him cry out, "Father, forgive them; for they do not know what they are doing" (Luke 23:34). But they had very different responses to him. All four Gospels tell us that Jesus was flanked by these two criminals, but only Luke tells us the conversations they had.

From the conversation that took place, we see that one man's heart was hard. Even as he hung on a cross naked and dying, he attempted to validate himself by joining the crowd in making Jesus feel small. He looked at Jesus and saw a failed

Messiah—a man who naively, even ludicrously, called people to love their enemies and to turn the other cheek; a man who, though he claimed to be the Messiah, refused to take up arms and fight the Romans. This criminal was angry when he heard Jesus pray, "Father, forgive them."

But something was happening to the heart of the other criminal as he watched and listened to Jesus on the cross. At some point he stopped hurling insults and spoke up, rebuking the other criminal. Perhaps as he reflected on what Jesus had said and what he had prayed, he began to think to himself, *My life is hopeless right now. I'm going to die in a matter of hours, humiliated and defeated. But maybe, just maybe, Jesus might be my hope. Maybe there really is a God who loves us. Maybe there is a God who cares for the hopeless. Maybe there is a God who gives second chances.* So he said to the other criminal, "Do you not fear God, since you are under the same sentence of condemnation? And we indeed have been condemned justly, for we are getting what we deserve for our deeds, but this man has done nothing wrong" (Luke 23:40-41). Then, whether from an emerging faith and understanding of what Jesus was doing or from a sense of compassion that prompted him to attempt to encourage Jesus, he spoke to Jesus and said, "Jesus, remember me when you come into your kingdom" (23:42).

Richard John Neuhaus reminds us in his book *Death on a Friday Afternoon: Meditations on the Last Words of Jesus from the Cross* that *remember* is a loaded word. "Remember me" meant "help me and deliver me." In the Old Testament, when God remembered individuals, God delivered them. In Genesis 8:1, God remembered Noah and saved him from the flood. In Genesis 19:29, God remembered Abraham, and therefore spared his nephew, Lot, from the destruction of Sodom and Gomorrah. In Genesis 30:22, God remembered Rachel and opened her womb so she could have a child. In Exodus 2:24, God remembered his covenant with Abraham and therefore delivered the Israelites from slavery in Egypt.

The bandit on the cross said, "Jesus, remember me when you come into your kingdom" (Luke 23:42). He was saying, "Deliver me from the place of the dead. Deliver me from the prison I am destined for. Remember me as the one who turned to you on the cross."

In this world there are some who, when they consider Jesus on the cross, see nothing more than a disillusioned man dying—a naive, sad, weak man; and they reject him. But others see in Jesus love embodied—God incarnate giving his life to get through to the human race; God freely laying down his life to take upon himself the poison of the world's sin; God seeking to reveal to the world the depth of God's love. Such individuals see in the cross hope for salvation and a second chance.

Two criminals. Two responses. The question we must ask ourselves is this: "Which thief will *I* be?"

A Simple but Significant Statement

Jesus listened to the second criminal's plea and replied to the thief, "Truly I tell you, today you will be with me in Paradise" (Luke 23:43). From this one simple statement, we can learn important truths about life after death, God's mercy, and heaven. Let's examine the statement more closely.

The Peace of Jesus' Words: "Today . . ."

What did Jesus mean by the word *today*? Some have suggested that it was a reference to when Jesus was speaking, not to when the man would be with him in paradise—as if Jesus was saying, "Today I tell you . . . someday you will be with me in paradise." But why would Jesus need to say, "Today I am telling you"? That doesn't make sense to me. I think he was meaning to say exactly what most translators have recorded: *"Today* you will be with me in Paradise."

The question is often asked, "Exactly what happens to us when we die?" The confusion comes in trying to put together those biblical passages that seem to point to a future day when the Resurrection will occur and Christ will judge the dead—such as some of Jesus' parables and Paul's writings in 1 Corinthians 15 and 1 Thessalonians 4—with those passages that speak of the dead being present with the Lord—such as Moses and Elijah appearing to Jesus (Matthew 17:3 and Luke 9:30), Paul expressing confidence in facing death because he will be with Christ (2 Corinthians 5:8), and Jesus' promise that the thief on the cross will be with him in paradise *today* (Luke 23:43).

After thirty years of study, my own view of what happens to us when we die is shaped by this passage and several others in the Bible. I believe that when we die, we immediately enter into Christ's kingdom—we are raised to life. I believe this because Jesus is recorded as having conversations with Moses and Elijah in the Gospels. I believe this because Paul noted that if he died he would be with the Lord, and his statement seems to indicate this would happen immediately. I believe this because Jesus turned to the thief on the cross and promised him that "today you will be with me in Paradise." I also believe this because of the near-death experiences of some people I've known, as well as the post-death experiences of people whose family members have died. I think of E.U., who, as he was approaching death, asked me if I could see all the people in the room with us. As far as I could see, we were alone. But E.U. was aware of a crowd of people I could not see who had died years before. I believe when we die we immediately go to be with Christ because of Ruth's grandmother, who, just before her death, awoke from her coma and looked at her grand-daughter and said, "Ruth, it's absolutely beautiful!" and then lay down and died. And I've got dozens of other stories like these.

Jesus' use of the word *today* is reassuring and comforting to us. Even so, this reassurance is not the primary point of Jesus' statement to the thief on the cross. So, what is the point of Jesus' words, "Today you will be with me in Paradise"?

The Point of Jesus' Words: "You Will Be With Me"

The foremost point of Jesus' words to the thief on the cross is to demonstrate the great mercy that God shows. Luke, whose focus throughout his Gospel is on Jesus' concern for the nobodies and the ne'er-do-wells and the sinners, wants us to see that even as a criminal was dying for his crimes, Jesus offered salvation.

We would do well to notice that Jesus didn't say, "Before I can offer you salvation, I need to make sure you fully understand some things: Do you believe in the Trinity? Do you believe that I am fully God and fully human? Do you believe the Bible is the inerrant, infallible Word of God? Have you been baptized? Have you accepted me into your heart?" No! Jesus saw that this man was reaching toward him, and he offered him paradise.

I'm not suggesting that understanding Christian doctrine and being baptized are not important; but what we see here is that Jesus looked at a man who had just turned to him in that moment, and that was enough. This man did not know Christian doctrine. But he had faith the size of a mustard seed, and that was enough for Jesus to say, "Today you will be with me in Paradise."

We Christians are good at making decisions for God about all the people we think aren't going to be in heaven. But how many of those people have as much faith and Christian doctrine as the thief on the cross did? Who are we to say that Jesus' words to the dying thief on the cross do not reflect the heart with which Jesus—who is the final judge before whom we will stand on Judgment Day—will judge us? I pray to God that this is precisely how he will look at us: looking beyond all that we have done wrong and setting aside our misconceptions and misunderstandings and faulty theology, he will see that we longed to be with him and that we put our trust in him. That will be enough, for as Paul notes, "We are saved by grace, through faith, and this not of ourselves, it is the gift of God." (See Ephesians 2:8.)

This thief had faith the size of a mustard seed, and it was enough. The good news is that God shows the same great mercy to each of us.

We see in Jesus' dying words what we see throughout his life: He wanted to save. He came proclaiming a God of the second chance.

This thief had faith the size of a mustard seed, and it was enough. The good news is that God shows the same great mercy to each of us.

The Promise of Jesus' Words: "In Paradise"

Finally, let's consider what Jesus' words tell us about heaven. Jesus said, "Today you will be with me in Paradise." The Greek word for *Paradise* in this verse is a transliteration of a Persian word that was used in ancient times to refer to the king's garden. The king's garden was a walled garden that was a place of profound beauty. Sometimes it included a menagerie—like a zoo—combined with beautiful gardens, trees, and water features. When someone was honored in ancient Persia, they were given the privilege of enjoying the king's garden.

I love this picture of Paradise—the King's Garden. Through Jesus Christ, we are invited to enter the garden, to savor his paradise. I have been several places in my life that I would call paradise. They were so awesomely beautiful they seemed almost unreal. Recently, my wife, LaVon, and I stayed several days in Sedona, Arizona, with the beautiful red rock mountains all around us. LaVon got tired of me repeatedly saying, "This is the most beautiful place I've ever been." She commented, "You say that about every beautiful place we've been." She's right! But as I climbed the red rocks and hiked up their trails, I felt such peace; my heart was filled with a sense of awe and joy.

The thought of spending eternity in the King's Garden with people I love, without hate or violence or stress or anxiety, sounds like paradise to me.

There was a doctor who made house calls back in the day when that was what doctors did. He took his dog with him in his horse and buggy. One day he visited a dying man, and as he went into the man's house, he left his dog on the front step. The dying man said to the doctor, "Doc, what's it going to be like—heaven—what will it be like?" At that moment the doctor's dog began to scratch at the door, whimpering and whining to get in. The doc stopped and said, "Do you hear that?" "Yes," the man replied. The doctor continued, "That's my dog. He has never been inside your house. He doesn't know what's on the other side of this door. All he knows is that his master is in here, and if his master is in here, it must be okay."

The Bible is surprisingly sparse in its descriptions of heaven. The Book of Revelation gives us a few glimpses, but it often speaks in symbolic language we're not meant to take literally. What we do know is that Jesus describes heaven as the King's Gardens—paradise—and we know that he, our master, will be there, so it must be okay.

Over time the word *paradise* came to be used of the garden of Eden by the Jewish people. Eden was, after all, the King's Garden—the garden of God. Adam and Eve were expelled from the garden because they disobeyed God, and human beings were forbidden from ever entering that garden again. Paradise was lost to humankind.

John's Gospel tells us that Jesus prayed in the garden of Gethsemane, was crucified in a garden at Calvary, and was buried in a garden next to Calvary. John tells us that when Jesus was raised from the dead, Mary Magdalene saw him and thought he was a gardener. This is important. What I believe John was saying, and what I believe Luke is hinting at in these

Through his suffering, death, and resurrection, Jesus was removing the curse that had banished humankind from the garden, from paradise, and he was inviting us to return to paradise with him.

words of Jesus spoken to a dying criminal, is that Jesus was opening the door to the King's Garden once more. Through his suffering, death, and resurrection, Jesus was removing the curse that had banished humankind from the garden, from paradise, and he was inviting us to return to paradise with him. And the first person he invited to join him in paradise was a hardened criminal, a thief on the cross.

"Today you will be with me in Paradise." These words of Jesus from the cross point us toward his mission—and ours: to seek and to save those who are lost. This includes those who, to us, seem to be hopelessly lost. These words beckon us to be like the thief whose heart was moved by seeing the crucified Jesus, and to pray with him, "Jesus, remember me when you come into your kingdom." These words point us toward the paradise that was restored by Jesus on the cross and remind us of the promise we have of dwelling in the King's Garden with him.

———————

Jesus, remember me when you come into your kingdom. I want to be with you in paradise. Help me to reach out to and love nonreligious and nominally religious people so that they might see your love through me. Amen.

3.

"Behold Your Son . . . Behold Your Mother"

Now there stood by the cross of Jesus His mother, and His mother's sister, Mary the wife of Clopas, and Mary Magdalene. When Jesus therefore saw His mother, and the disciple whom He loved standing by, He said to His mother, "Woman, behold your son!" Then He said to the disciple, "Behold your mother!" And from that hour that disciple took her to his own home. (John 19:25-27 NKJV)

Mary the Wife of Clopas

I begged her not to follow as Jesus was led to be crucified. "Mary, it will be too hard. You don't want to see this." But she said to me, "I will not let my son die alone among these wolves." And so we went, joined by only one of his disciples, the young John, and by Mary of Magdala.

Jesus' mother was a strong and determined woman. And she loved her son as much as any woman ever loved a son. He was to her the joy of her life and the purpose of her existence. Jesus had sought to prepare her for what lay ahead in Jerusalem. Somehow she had always known he would die as a young man, giving his life to save the world.

Mary was determined to stand near Jesus as he suffered. She would fight to hold back the tears, seeking to show her son strength and love. She would do all she could, standing there, to ease his pain and to give him hope.

As the crowd hurled their insults, Mary slowly pushed her way through until she stood before him. There he hung, naked so as to humiliate and in wretched pain. Jesus' feet were two feet off the ground, and from where Mary stood she could reach up and touch his chest, though the Roman guards forbade such things. As we stood there, Mary said to Jesus, "I love you, my son. Your Father will soon come for you. You are in his hands. I love you."

It was then that Jesus looked at his mother and spoke slowly and tenderly to her, "Dear woman, this now is your son." He nodded his head toward John. And then, to John he said, "Here is your mother." John placed his arm around Mary and held her as if to say to Jesus, "I understand, I will take care of her."

No mother should have to watch her son die the agonizing death of crucifixion.

The third time that Jesus spoke from the cross, he spoke to his mother and his closest disciple, John, in a scene that is both moving and filled with import for the Christian life. In this chapter I invite you to consider five ways in which these final words of Jesus speak to us today.

The Role of Women in Jesus' Ministry

Let's consider the fact that there were three women standing at the foot of the cross with Jesus as he suffered and died. John tells us they were Mary the mother of Jesus; her sister, Mary the wife of Clopas; and Mary of Magdala. John also notes that he himself stood with these women—the lone disciple to be present—while the other disciples remained at some distance, fearing for their lives. Two of these women are familiar to us, but who was Mary the wife of Clopas?

John describes Mary the wife of Clopas as the sister of Mary. The early church noted that she was Mary's sister by marriage, as Clopas was the brother of Joseph, the earthly father of Jesus. Joseph likely died when Jesus was a young man (the last we hear of him in the Gospels is when Jesus was twelve). It also is likely that, since Joseph's death, Clopas had provided support and care for Joseph's wife, Mary, and her children. Undoubtedly Clopas's wife, Mary, was a close companion and friend to her sister-in-law, and she is the only friend Mary had who stood with her that day. We learn from the early church fathers that Clopas and Mary's son, Symeon—Jesus' cousin—went on to become the leader of the church of Jerusalem after the deaths of James and Peter.

As I consider these three women standing in the midst of this hostile crowd, I'm struck by the role women played in Jesus' ministry. It was the women who financially supported the work of Jesus and the disciples (Luke 8:1-3). It was a woman who became the first missionary to the Samaritans (John 4:28-29). It was a woman who anointed Jesus with oil in preparation for his death (Matthew 26:6-13). It was three women who had the courage to stand by Jesus' cross for six hours as he died (John 19:25). It was women who first came to the tomb and found it empty on Easter morning (Mark 16:1-8). It was a woman who first saw Christ raised from the dead and, in turn, a woman who became the first to proclaim the Resurrection to others (John 20:11-18). Jesus regularly showed compassion, mercy, and love toward women in the Gospels, which stood out as counter-cultural in his day.

Jesus' choice of twelve men as his formal "disciples" and Paul's commands restricting the role of teacher within the church to men were signs of first-century cultural norms—it was men alone who were rabbis in their time—but both Jesus and Paul recognized the giftedness, courage, and commitment of women in the early church. Thankfully, we live in a day and time when these cultural norms are no longer in place. Today many of the most effective preachers, teachers, and leaders in the church are women. Their leadership is in a long tradition that began with these biblical women who followed and supported the ministry of Jesus and who courageously stood with him during those final hours of his life.

Mary as the Second Eve

As we consider the role of these other women in the life of Jesus, we recognize that Mary the mother of Jesus is the single most important human being to God's saving plans aside from Jesus himself. It was Mary who, when called to risk her life and give up all of her dreams in order to carry, deliver, and raise the Messiah, replied, "Here I am, the servant of the Lord; let it be with me according to your word" (Luke 1:38).

It was Mary who carried the Son of God in her womb, having supplied the human material needed for the Incarnation; her body and blood nourished and nurtured God's Word as it was becoming flesh. No other human being has ever had such an intimate relationship to God. Theologians of the Church called her *Theotokos*, meaning the God-bearer, since it was she who gave birth to God enfleshed.

This woman who stood by the cross seeking desperately to console and give hope to her dying son paid a great price for our salvation. I have on many occasions told my children that I would give my life for them without hesitating. Surely Mary felt the same as she stood there that day. It was not only Jesus who suffered for the salvation of the world. Mary, too, suffered for us as she stood by those six hours, watching him die.

Throughout the history of the Christian faith, Mary has been seen as a second Eve. Through the first Eve, paradise was lost, but through the Gift born of Mary, the second Eve, paradise was restored.

Honor Your Father and Your Mother

Perhaps the most common understanding of this passage is that even as he hung on the cross dying in pain, Jesus was concerned for his mother. While Mary stood there, seeking to comfort and console her son, Jesus, even as life ebbed from him, sought to ensure his mother would be taken care of after he was gone. And so he asked John to care for his mother, and he asked his mother to accept John's protection and care.

According to one tradition in the church, Mary lived out her days with John in the town of Ephesus on the west coast of what is now Turkey. You can even visit what some believe was the home John built for Mary and the place she lived until the end of her life (though a much earlier tradition says Mary lived out her days in Jerusalem).

John makes clear in his prologue that Jesus is God's Word made flesh—that in his words and his life we see and understand God and God's will for humankind. In this tender conversation we see the fifth commandment, God's call for humanity to honor our mothers and our fathers. To honor them is to ensure that they are cared for.

It was in reflecting upon these words that a friend of mine told me, "God convicted me about my need to do more to care for my own mother. I began in earnest to consider her needs for companionship and for financial help when she retires. I was convicted that my mom needed more from me than I had been providing up to that point." He saw in this passage Jesus modeling for him the role he was to play for his own mother.

We live in a day and time when many of our parents may not have adequately prepared for retirement. I was born in 1964, the last year of the baby boom. My parents were born in 1946, the first year of the baby boom! According to a recent survey of workers fifty-five and older, 36 percent had saved less than $25,000 for retirement.[2] As pensions disappear and Social Security benefits seem likely to decrease while medical costs increase, we need to reclaim what was the practice throughout most of human history: caring for one's parents as Jesus was asking John to do for his mother.

John as a Model for the Church

Some believe that by relating these words of Jesus, John intends more than a simple witness for us to care for our parents. Fleming Rutledge says that both the disciple and Mary "represent the way that family ties are transcended in the church by the ties of the Spirit."[3] She notes how, in John's Gospel, there is usually a deeper meaning to his stories. In this case, John intends us to understand from Jesus that, as his disciples, we are responsible to care for one another, even taking on the role of parent or child or brother or sister to another who needs us.

Roger is an elementary school teacher in Manhattan, Kansas. One night many years ago, Roger was working late. As he was leaving the school building long after dark, he noticed one of his students, a boy named Johnathon, swinging on the playground by himself. He asked the fourth-grader why he was at the playground so late on a school night and learned that this little boy's mother had left the family and that his father worked all night and struggled to care for him. Roger showed compassion and reassured Johnathon that things would be okay; then he sent the boy home. Roger took a special interest in Johnathon and began to look for ways to help him. Within the year Johnathon was placed in a foster home as his father was unable to care for him. He eventually returned to his father's home, but once more his father was unable to care for him. Knowing

As his disciples, we are responsible to care for one another, even taking on the role of parent or child or brother or sister to another who needs us.

Johnathon would be sent back to a foster home, his father asked the elementary school teacher if he would take Johnathon into his home. Roger agreed and welcomed this child as if he were his own son. His role in caring for, mentoring, and shaping Johnathon's life gave Johnathon a radically different future than he might have had.

Johnathon was a gifted child who grew up to be a remarkable man. With the help of Roger, he went to Kansas State University. He travelled across the country and to different parts of the world. He fell in love with a beautiful young woman and married her, and together they went to serve the poor in South Africa before returning to Chicago, where he works with inner-city boys who have no place to call home.

Johnathon and Roger's story is particularly important to me, because the woman Johnathon married is my daughter. From the day Danielle was born, I began to pray for the boy who one day would be her husband. Little did I know I was praying for a little boy whose troubled life would find stability and joy and a future with hope because of the love of a teacher whose faith compelled him to see this child as his own. How grateful I am that Roger had heard the words spoken from the cross, "Behold your son."

The church I serve has a partnership with seven inner-city schools. These schools did not have playgrounds, so we built them playgrounds. We provide tutors for students needing additional help and class parties for students with perfect attendance. We repaint and repair the schools. We provide book fairs, school supplies, and winter clothes. And for those children who do not have enough to eat at home, we provide backpacks with nutritious snacks for the weekends. Recently

I received a notebook filled with handwritten thank-you notes from the children at one of the elementary schools. Here are a couple of the notes:

> Dear Church of the Resurrection,
> Thank you for the coat because I didn't have a coat. This one is comfortable and very warm. Also, thank you for the holiday parties.

> Dear Church of the Resurrection,
> Thank you so much for the tutoring program. It really helped me get my work right. Thanks to you I'm smarter than ever, thank you! And thank you for the playground! We never had one before. I really like the swings. You have done so much and all I can say is "Thank You!"

At the end of the past school year, we provided a skating party for the children as a way of celebrating their accomplishments. Many of the kids had never been skating. I was struck by something one boy said in his note:

> Dear Church of the Resurrection,
> Thank you for the snacks we take home on the weekend, and for writing to us as pen pals. And thank you for paying for our skating party. When I got to the skating rink I did not know how to skate. I would fall sometimes but I had a great time. I wish you could have been there to see us dancing too. *Even the teachers were dancing*.

It was that last line that got me. I could picture these teachers who work in schools challenged by poverty and inadequate resources dancing with their children. To me this was a picture of the kingdom of God—*"even the teachers were dancing."* That's what happens when the church follows Jesus' call to "behold your child."

Many others in our church have heard Jesus' words to his disciple John, "Behold your mother," and have taken them to heart.

Fay is one of those people. She began volunteering in our ministry for seniors. She went out of her way to care for them. One ninety-five-year-old woman cried when Fay placed a birthday crown upon her head. It was her first birthday party in ninety years. One of the women who attended this group was Bettie, a member of our church whose Alzheimer's was advancing. Fay came to love her as though she were her own mother. She would visit in Bettie's home, kneeling down next to her with joy to talk with her. Bettie always responded with a huge smile whenever Fay drew near. As I was writing this chapter, Bettie died. Over the days leading up to her death, Fay was there every day, speaking tenderly to her, holding her hand, and continuing to love her. Fay heard the call of Jesus, "Behold your mother."

Hundreds of people in the church I serve have intentionally developed caring relationships with people who are older or younger than they are. Several years ago Ray's wife, Betty, died. Ray and Betty had been married more than sixty years. Some worried about what would happen to Ray without Betty there. But Ray had invested in the lives of so many younger people, encouraging them, mentoring them, and blessing them. This is what had kept him young all those years. Now he had no shortage of people who knew it was time to return the favor. Ray worships at our Saturday-night service, and each week when I look out where he is sitting, I see friends who are his age and people who are twenty and thirty years younger than he is making sure that he knows he is loved and is never alone.

The idea that relationships in the church transcend family relationships becomes even clearer when we consider Jesus' words, "Whoever does the will of God is my brother and sister and mother" (Mark 3:35). Penny Ellwood, one of the pastors I serve with at Resurrection, noted that at the foot of the cross, John assumed responsibility to care for someone that Jesus cared for deeply. John would open his home and devote his time and resources to care for Mary. In doing so, both John and Mary would model for us the call of Christ to see those in need as our mother or father or son or daughter.

A Woman Who Lost a Son

Robbie's thirty-one-year-old son died ten years ago in a tragic accident. One Advent I was preaching a series of sermons about Mary, and Robbie said to me, "Adam, I've never told anyone this, but every time you preach about Mary, I feel a connection to her. I feel I know what she must have experienced in the death of her son. And she must know what I have experienced." She went on to describe for me her feelings after the loss of her son: "When you lose a child, you lose part of yourself as a woman. He was inside you. He was your flesh and blood. I feel Mary's pain, having lost a son. It is absolutely catastrophic devastation at first." I asked Robbie to tell me, as a mother who lost a son, how she imagined Mary felt in the years after Jesus' death, and this is what she said to me:

I'm sure she lived with a great sadness always, but because she loved her son so much and saw what he was trying to accomplish, I'm sure that was her mission in life—to carry on what he was trying to do in his life. She was a very brave and strong woman, obviously, for everything she went through, from when Christ was born till the very end of his life, too. I think she really knew she had a mission in life that God had given her, and she tried to carry that out her whole life.

John's inclusion of the story of Mary standing at the foot of the cross and watching Jesus die reminds us that the most important woman who ever lived, the woman who God loved and "highly favored," walked through the hell of losing a child. She came to understand the suffering of those who've lost a child. But Jesus did not intend for Mary's loss to be the end of her life. She had work yet to do, and her loss prepared her to care for others and to be a compelling witness to others for the rest of her life.

Robbie has lived this way too. After her son's death, she became even more involved in serving Christ and serving others. She has been a part of the parent's grief group at our church, she sings in the choir, she is one of the leaders of the cancer support group for women, and she serves in a myriad of other ways—all of which not only have helped her in her own grief but also have fulfilled God's vision for her life. She is one of Christ's witnesses.

In this scene and in these final words, we see the courage of the women who were a part of Jesus' life and ministry. We are reminded once more of the profound role that Mary played in God's redemptive work through Jesus Christ. We recall Jesus' witness and call to care for our parents. We see a picture of what it means to be the church— **Jesus' words . . . remind us that this mission is ours, as well—caring for those Jesus cares for as if they are our own family.** Christians caring for those who are younger and those who are older, as though those in need were our children or our parents. And we see in Mary one who, though favored by God, walked through this dark valley but—as Jesus himself expected her to do—carried on Christ's mission after he was gone. Jesus' words to "Behold your son" and "Behold your mother" remind us that this mission is ours, as well—caring for those Jesus cares for as if they are our own family.

Lord, thank you for your mother, Mary. Her witness, courage, and love for you were most profound. Help me to heed your call to John and to hear it as my own, so that I might care for my parents and children, and so that I might see those who have no parent or child as my own parents and children and care for them. Amen.

4.

"My God, My God, Why Have You Forsaken Me?"

Those who passed by derided him, shaking their heads and saying, "Aha! You who would destroy the temple and build it in three days, save yourself, and come down from the cross!" In the same way the chief priests, along with the scribes, were also mocking him among themselves and saying, "He saved others; he cannot save himself. Let the Messiah, the King of Israel, come down from the cross now, so that we may see and believe." Those who were crucified with him also taunted him.

When it was noon, darkness came over the whole land until three in the afternoon. At three o'clock Jesus cried out with a loud voice, "Eloi, Eloi, lema sabachthani?" which means, "My God, my God, why have you forsaken me?" When some of the bystanders heard it, they said, "Listen, he is calling for Elijah." And someone ran, filled a sponge with sour wine, put it on a stick, and gave it to him to drink.

(Mark 15:29-36a)

A Man in the Crowd

It was a morbid sense of curiosity that made us stop. We were on our way to the city on the first day of the festival when we noticed the crowd watching as three men hung nailed to Roman crosses. It was a gruesome way to die: hanging by the hands and feet—with the added humiliation of being stripped of clothing—and slowly dying as breathing became increasingly impossible. For all its horror, we were drawn to take a closer look at the suffering inflicted on these men.

I was embarrassed to be watching yet unable to turn away. It was clear as I looked at the crowd that there was something unusual about the man in the center. Some were hurling insults at him. Three women stood weeping near him. He'd clearly been flogged—the bloodied stripes giving witness to the cruelty of his captors. I asked what had he done wrong? Someone in the crowd answered, "That's Jesus, the man from Galilee, who many believed would lead the revolt to expel the Romans. But his way of dealing with the Romans was to tell his followers to show them kindness! He seemed more intent on revolting against the Sanhedrin. It was they who convinced Pilate that he was a threat to Roman rule. So here we are with a pacifist preacher crucified as a threat to the Emperor!"

The crowd around Jesus was restless. Some of the merchants seemed to gloat that he who had cast them out of the Temple courts a few days earlier was now getting his "just reward." I'd like to say that as we watched this scene unfold, our hearts were filled with compassion, but it was quite the opposite. The anger and venom of the others was like an infection, rapidly spreading to each of us. My friend Levi was the first to join in the act, saying, "He got what he had coming to him. He preached salvation, but look at him now. This friend of drunkards and prostitutes couldn't save a soul!"

My friend Jacob looked up at Jesus and shouted, "Who do you think you are anyway? Some kind of Messiah you've turned out to be. Look at you—naked, bleeding, dying!" Levi picked up the refrain, "I'm sick just looking at you. Get it over with already!" As I listened to them shouting, hate began to well up in me. This man hadn't done anything to me, yet as the others were shouting I found myself filled with anger. I walked up to him and said, "Some Jew you are. You make me sick! Tell us to love our enemies! This is what happens to people who love their enemies! Listen, you're a nobody!" And then I spat on him.

I don't know why I did it. He hadn't done anything to me. In fact, by all accounts he was a good man. But somehow, hearing the priests and religious leaders mocking him, my friends hurling insults at him, and even the thief on the cross next to him maligning him, a kind of evil seized my heart. I discovered that day that I had the capacity to hate an innocent man and a sick desire to be a part of making him hurt.

It was after I shouted at him that he looked up to the heavens and shouted the words of the psalmist: "My God, my God, why have you forsaken me?" When I heard him cry out, I was filled with shame. My God, what had we done?

The Gospels record seven last statements of Jesus. Luke and John each record three, but Matthew's and Mark's Gospels only tell us of one statement that Jesus made from the cross. He surely said more, but for these two Gospel writers, this one statement was all that needed to be recorded. For many, it is the most moving, disturbing, and powerfully haunting statement of the seven: "My God, my God, why have you forsaken me?" These words reflect not only the darkness of the horrific experience Jesus endured, but also the darkness within those who surrounded Jesus at the foot of the cross. Yet as we study the psalm Jesus was praying, we will discover that those words may point to a deeper faith that sustained him in his suffering on the cross.

The Mob Mentality

Before Jesus uttered his "cry of dereliction," the Roman soldiers had mistreated and maligned him. The crowd had mocked him relentlessly. Passersby had derided him. The chief priests and scribes had insulted him. Those who were crucified beside him had taunted him. It was not enough that they had crucified Jesus; they wanted to destroy him—to crush him and to dehumanize him.

It would be easy for us to think that all of those involved in dehumanizing Jesus were horrible people. If it were only the Roman soldiers, we might say, "Well, the Roman soldiers did terrible things like that." Or if it were just the thieves on either side of Jesus, we could say, "After all, they were criminals. That's what you would expect." But the people who led the charge in dehumanizing and humiliating Jesus were considered the most pious people on the face of the planet in that day. They were deeply committed Jews, including religious leaders. They were the priests and the scribes. The scribes were those who copied

The people who led the charge in dehumanizing and humiliating Jesus were considered the most pious people on the face of the planet in that day.

the Scriptures from generation to generation, studied and interpreted the Scriptures, and gave legal rulings based on the Scriptures. A modern-day equivalent might be Bible scholars and pastors who have been to seminary, or dedicated lay-persons who have committed themselves to ongoing, in-depth Bible study and Scripture memorization. That was the kind of people who were humiliating Jesus.

It was not enough that they had conspired with the Romans to silence Jesus and see him crucified. It was not enough that they wanted Jesus to die from the most cruel and inhumane form of capital punishment ever invented by human beings. They also sought to humiliate him and to crush his spirit as he hung there. This is what they were doing as they hurled their insults at him.

In addition to the religious leaders, there also were the passersby—those who were going into or out of the city. They, too, joined in, hurling insults at Jesus. These bystanders were Jewish people who had come to Jerusalem to celebrate the Passover. The previous night they had eaten the roasted lamb they had offered in sacrifice to God; they had told the story of how God had saved their people from slavery in Egypt; they had placed a cup for Elijah on the table, anticipating the coming of the Messiah; and they had drunk from that cup, hoping and praying for the coming of the Messiah. Then, after the Passover meal, they had sung the Hallel Psalm: "Give thanks to the LORD, for he is good; his love endures forever" (Psalm 106:1 NIV).

How could anyone sing a song of praise such as this and then spew hurtful, hateful words at the man whose so-called crimes were healing the sick on the sabbath and claiming to be God's Messiah? Again, we are tempted to say, "Well, those were first-century Jews. They were not Christians like us. *We* would never say anything so hurtful. We would never treat anyone so uncharitably. We would never do evil such as that." *Really?*

It has been said that, in the trial and crucifixion of Jesus, it was not Jesus who was on trial but humanity. This scene with the passersby hurling insults at Jesus points to something dreadfully wrong with us. Rather than feeling compassion, the passersby found the suffering of this man moved them to cruelty and hate. And this was not simply a problem with the first-century Jews who stood by the cross. The scene holds a mirror to our own souls. We're meant to see ourselves in the crowd, and it's not that hard to do. The problem is within us, and it begins at a very young age.

When I was in the fourth grade, my mother came home from work one day after she had been shopping for new underwear for me. They were Jockey briefs, and they were different colors. I remember one of the colors was a kind of golden or copper color. As she handed them to me she said, "I bought these for you, because I knew you needed new underwear." I replied, "Mom, these are colored. I can't wear these." "Oh, they're the stylish thing now, Adam," she said. I repeated that I would not wear them. "Yes, you will," she insisted. "I bought them for you, and you're going to wear them." So I decided I had better get it over with and wear them.

I put the golden underwear on first, and I wore them to school. What I didn't realize was that it was gym day. So I went into the locker room and I waited until everyone else had left the room to pull off my jeans and put on my gym shorts. But there was one kid who had stayed behind, and he saw my golden underwear.

Already I was taunted regularly with comments such as, "One-Adam-Twelve, One-Adam-Twelve" (from the 70's TV show *Adam Twelve*), or "Adam, where's Eve?" And because I had bright orange hair at the time, kids would sometimes say, "I'd rather be dead than have red on the head." Now I was going to be known for my golden underwear!

We left the locker room and joined our gym class, and, of course, that kid proceeded to tell everybody in the class that I was wearing golden underwear. Only one or two hours after gym class, every kid in the fourth grade knew I was wearing golden underwear. It's funny now; it wasn't funny then. At that point it was the worst day of my life.

When it came time for recess, I knew what was going to happen: I would be tortured on the playground. Naturally I was relieved when I got there and saw that two girls were already being picked on by a group of kids. So, I joined in. I was so glad that they were getting picked on, because it meant nobody was going to pick on *me*. One of the girls' parents ended up withdrawing her from school before the end of the year because she always was being tortured and tormented by the other kids.

You probably remember the kid who was picked on in your school. Perhaps it was you sometimes. Maybe you were glad to be the one picking on someone else. At one time or another, we all are party to this kind of childhood harassment. Then, as we get older, we become more sophisticated in the ways we hurt others.

In recent years, there have been several publicized cases of cyber bullying that have resulted in suicides. Reports of harassment, assault, violence, murder, terrorism, and war are in the news every day. We see the dark side. We know it exists. Carl Jung called it the shadow; Christians speak of it as our sin nature. Whatever you call it, it lurks in our hearts from the time we are young, waiting to be ignited by a spark.

Aleksandr Solzhenitsyn, who spent years in a Soviet prison camp, wrote in his most famous book, *The Gulag Archipelago*, these words:

> If only there were evil people somewhere insidiously committing evil deeds, and it were necessary only to separate them from the rest of us and destroy them. But the line dividing good and evil cuts through the heart of every human being. And who is willing to destroy a piece of his own heart?[4]

The impulses that led the Germans to murder millions of Jews, the Soviets to murder millions of their own people, the Khmer Rouge to murder millions of Cambodians, and the Hutu of Rwanda to take machetes to 800,000 of their fellow church members, co-workers, and neighbors who were Tutsi, exist in all of us. Yet we are surprised to hear that many of the people involved in these unforgettable atrocities claimed to be Christians. We wonder how they could unleash such terrible disasters and think we would never do anything so horrible.

When I look at our country and see the way we are so divided, I wonder what it would take to move one segment of our population to justify violence against another segment. We've seen acts of violence against immigrants. We've had political rallies where people show up with guns. Politicians have been shot, gay and lesbian people have been beaten, and students have plotted to blow up their schools. There is darkness inside each of us.

If these previous examples seem too dramatic for you, consider what makes you explode in rage, leads you to say hurtful words about others, or causes you to act in unchristian ways. If it is not politics or religion or fear, perhaps it is being told "no"—not getting your way. That brings it closer to home.

We are used to getting our way, and we don't like it when someone tells us "no." In fact, we hate to be told no. So, when the sales clerk tells us that we can't return something, or when the waiter or waitress tells us we can't have something, we explode in anger and make the other person feel small.

Surely no *Christians* ever do that, right? Regrettably, we know the truth.

When I was a youth pastor, I was having lunch with an associate pastor of a church. I watched as he exploded at the waitress when he didn't get his way. I couldn't believe it. But did I stand up for her and speak to this pastor? No. I just sat there, silently hoping he would stop.

Selfishness, pride, fear, and ignorance so easily lead to rage and hate. We see others as worthy of our scorn—or worse, our cruelty and injustice—and so we dehumanize them. This is how the shadow within us works, and it is a part of each of us—this tendency to demonize those who see the world differently, who look different, or whose views on anything from how to interpret the Bible to politics or economics are different from our own.

We must ask ourselves, *What is it that leads me to dehumanize others—in essence, to join the crowd of the religious people who stood around Jesus to humiliate him?* Once we see ourselves in the crowd, we're prepared to actually hear these haunting words of Jesus from the cross: "My God, my God, why have you forsaken me?"

From that vantage point, let us now consider three things that Jesus' words tell us about him—and about us.

Jesus Knows What It's Like to Feel Abandoned by God

The cry "My God, my God, why have you forsaken me?" sometimes is called the "cry of dereliction" or cry of abandonment. In that moment, as Jesus prayed these words, Jesus Christ, the Son of God and the Savior of the world, felt abandoned or forsaken by God. This thought can be confusing in light of our Trinitarian theology, which asserts that the Father, Son, and Spirit are one. While I do not completely understand this myself, it seems clear to me that as he hung on the cross, Jesus no longer felt the presence of his Father. He felt alone and abandoned.

Some believe that Luke and John did not include this passage in their accounts of the Crucifixion because it seemed to diminish the sense of the majesty or dignity of Jesus. Perhaps they worried that believers would be confused by the idea that Jesus felt abandoned by God. Yet it is precisely the dignity and majesty of Jesus that Matthew and Mark likely saw in this prayer. For them, Jesus the Lord was actually experiencing that feeling of God-forsakenness that every one of us experiences at some point in our lives. He knew what it was to feel that

God, his Father, had abandoned him. He knew what it was like to feel hopelessness and despair.

As a pastor I have often shared this story of Jesus with parishioners who were walking through dark valleys. I sat with a family after their teenage daughter had died. The pain and darkness were overwhelming. They felt God had abandoned them. It was to this story that we turned in Scripture to see that at the center of our faith was a man who was cruelly tortured and put to death at the age of thirty-three, and who, as he hung dying, felt abandoned by God. I invited them to pray to Jesus, the one who himself had experienced despair and darkness and who understood.

We all pray this prayer, "My God, my God, why have you forsaken me?" at some time in our lives—when someone we dearly love dies, when we find ourselves facing a battle we never wanted to face, when we've been humiliated and made to feel small. There are a thousand other ways we might experience a sense of being forsaken by God—times when God is conspicuously silent and absent. In those times, we can pray to Jesus Christ, because he knows what we are experiencing and feeling. We can pray to the One who sympathizes with us in that moment while, at the same time, saying, "God didn't forsake me, and God hasn't forsaken you." In his intellect, I'm sure that Jesus *knew* that God had not forsaken him. But in his heart, that's how he *felt*. And I am thankful that our Lord—our King—understands fully and completely what it feels like to feel forsaken by God.

We all pray this prayer, "My God, my God, why have you forsaken me?" at some time in our lives. . . . In those times, we can pray to Jesus Christ, because he knows what we are experiencing and feeling.

In the Spring of 2011—what became known as the Arab Spring—Arabs of several nations rose up against their leaders. They did so because their leaders, while living in wealth and splendor, were oblivious to the suffering and difficulties of the average person. In fact, the leaders contributed to this adversity. They seemed not to notice, understand, or care about the suffering of their people while they freely enriched themselves at the expense of their citizens. Jesus could have been this kind of king, a king who would utter decrees and live in the lap of luxury and avoid all kind of suffering. In fact, this was one of the three temptations the devil gave Jesus when he began his ministry: "Bow down and worship me, and I will give you all the riches of the world!" (Matthew 4:9, author's paraphrase). But this was not Jesus' way. As a king, he came to his people—particularly to those who suffered—seeking to heal and to deliver them. Ultimately, he faced grave injustice, suffering, torture, and death. He chose to identify with the suffering of his people. This is the kind of King we follow. And when we feel forsaken, hopeless, and in despair, we pray to one who walked this path before us.

I love Jesus for undergoing such a dreadful experience, for it tells me that he identifies with, understands, and has compassion on each of us when we walk through dark and difficult places.

Jesus Teaches Us to Suffer and Sacrifice for Others

Jesus' words also reveal true sacrificial love. Jesus' death was not painless and without suffering. No! Part of the mission he was pursuing and the gift he was offering was true suffering for us. He died so that the world might live, and in this mystery we see the costliness of grace. Jesus showed us by example what sacrificial, redemptive love looks like. Purposeful sacrifice to save others is costly—not only in time or money, but also in the emotional and spiritual suffering that comes when we give ourselves for others.

I am reminded of these words from one of the most powerful hymns of the cross, an American folk hymn sometimes attributed to Alexander Means entitled "What Wondrous Love Is This":

> What wondrous love is this, O my soul, O my soul!
> What wondrous love is this, O my soul!
> What wondrous love is this that caused the Lord of bliss
> To bear the dreadful curse for my soul, for my soul,
> To bear the dreadful curse for my soul.

The gospel calls us to a life in which we risk, sacrifice, and give ourselves so that others might know the love of God. Has the sharing of God's love cost you anything or given you any discomfort? Have you been willing to pay any price or to sacrifice anything for this call?

In the years when I was in seminary and worked as a youth pastor, I took youth on mission trips every year. One year we loaded a bus full of kids and drove to Hot Springs, Arkansas. Our youth raised $180 each and gave up a week of their summer vacation to take the trip. Our destination was an inner-city church. Almost all the members were elderly, and they were struggling to pay the bills. The bathrooms were in bad shape, and the paint was peeling off the ceiling. So we remodeled their bathrooms and repainted the sanctuary. We also went door to door inviting people to vacation Bible school, which we held on the church parking lot every evening.

On the last day we were there, I misplaced the folder that contained all the information related to the trip. One of the church members found it and brought it to me. She said, "Adam, is this your folder?" I said, "Oh, yes, I've been missing that. Thank you." She continued, "You know, I didn't know whose it was, and so I opened it and saw that there was a ledger sheet in there with all the kids' names and a dollar amount beside each. Did they really pay $180 each to come here to paint our sanctuary, fix our bathrooms, and do vacation Bible school for the neighborhood children?" I replied, "Yes, ma'am. They've been working for a long time to come here." She began to cry and said, "I can't believe a group of teenagers would love us so much that they would give so much to come and help us. What kind of people are these?" I said, "They're just Christians."

What these youth were doing is a fundamental part of the life of a Christian. As followers of a crucified Messiah, we are willing to do what is inconvenient, uncomfortable, sacrificial, and even risky in order to be a part of his redemptive work in the world. When lived out by ordinary Christians, this redemptive work looks like the guys in the church I serve who, after they get off work at their day jobs, show up to repair cars for people in the community who are struggling financially. It looks like the team of people who buy their own plane tickets and fly eighteen hours in order to go to one of the poorest countries in Africa to coordinate efforts to drill "bore holes" so that children are no longer made sick by the water they drink. It looks like the team of men and women who go to the Federal Penitentiary in Leavenworth to mentor people who have been written off as hopeless causes. It looks like the fifty-plus laypeople in our church who visit the hospitals when people are sick and who call upon the grieving and those who ask for prayer, offering them encouragement and care. Each of these individuals takes time away from working, watching television, playing golf, or taking a vacation in order to selflessly serve others.

I see this every day among Christians I know—people who routinely and voluntarily choose to take risks and set aside their own comfort and convenience in order to follow their crucified Messiah.

Jesus Prays and Worships in His Time of Despair

Finally, Jesus' words reveal that in the moment when he felt abandoned and forsaken by God, he chose to pray, for the "cry of dereliction" is actually the first verse of a psalm that Jesus must have been singing and praying from the cross.

What a contrast that is to the typical human response. When we experience tough times, we tend to become disappointed with God. Often we turn away from God, refusing to pray and pretending God doesn't exist. We decide we don't want anything to do with God because God didn't help us in the way we wanted. But Jesus didn't do that. Even though he was questioning God—"My God, my God, why have you forsaken me?"—he still was praying. Questioning God in prayer is an act of faith—even when there is confusion about what is happening.

Yet Jesus was doing more than praying. He was actually worshiping. The words "My God, my God, why have you forsaken me?"

Jesus was doing more than praying. He was actually worshiping.

are the first stanza of a hymn that most of the Jews in Jesus' day would have known: Psalm 22. The hymn begins,

> My God, my God, why have you forsaken me?
>   Why are you so far from helping me, from the words of
>   my groaning?
> O my God, I cry by day, but you do not answer;
>   and by night, but find no rest. (verses 1-2)

The Jews standing around the cross would have known this song. It would be like someone crying out "Amazing Grace, how sweet the sound" among a group of Christians; most would immediately think to themselves, "that saved a wretch like me." Jesus cited the first line, but he knew well the rest of the psalm.

Imagine you are with an elderly family member as she is dying, and you hear her whisper the first line of a hymn. Knowing that she didn't get a chance to say the rest of it, you would go to find out what else was in that hymn. If I were the pastor conducting the funeral, we would sing that hymn at her funeral; and I would talk about the fact that her dying words were from this hymn, which means that she was thinking about the hymn as she died.

Similarly, Jesus' words "My God, My God, why have you forsaken me?" tell us that he was thinking about the hymn that is Psalm 22 when he died. When we look at the words of the hymn, it's easy to understand why. The hymn goes on to describe a time when David was suffering at the hands of his enemies. There are interesting parallels with what was happening at the cross:

> All who see me mock at me. (verse 7)
> A company of evildoers encircles me. (verse 16)
> For my clothing they cast lots. (verse 18)
> They have pierced my hands and feet. (verse 16 NIV)

But the psalm doesn't end there. It would be a tragic hymn if it did, but it is not a hymn of despair. Though it begins darkly, throughout it affirms the psalmist's trust in God.

Just as we know that "Amazing Grace" ends with the hopeful vision of singing God's praise for all eternity, so the Jews at the foot of the cross knew that Psalm 22 ends not in a cry of dereliction, but in a note of confidence that God had not abandoned the psalmist. Consider verse 24:

> For he did not despise or abhor
>   the affliction of the afflicted;
> he did not hide his face from me,
>   but heard when I cried to him. (verse 24)

Is it possible that Jesus chose to pray the opening words of Psalm 22 as he suffered on the cross to point not only to his pain and despair but also to his trust that God had, in fact, heard him and would deliver him?

When we feel abandoned by God, we, too, must choose to trust that God has not really forsaken us. We must trust that God will not hide his face from us, and that God hears us when we pray. And that leads to confidence in a future yet unseen.

So, while Jesus suffered there upon the cross, preparing for his imminent death and burial, he likely recounted in his mind the final verses of Psalm 22:

> Before him shall bow all who go down to the dust,
>> and I shall live for him.
> Posterity will serve him;
>> future generations will be told about the Lord,
> and proclaim his deliverance to a people yet unborn.
>> (verses 29-32)

These words pointed to the confident hope that death would not be the end for the psalmist, death would not be the end for Jesus, and death certainly would not be the end for the gospel, for as the psalmist noted with confidence, "Future generations will be told about the Lord and proclaim his deliverance to a people yet unborn."

There are at least three things we are meant to remember when we hear Jesus praying from the cross, "My God, my God, why have you forsaken me?"

First, we are meant to find ourselves in the crowd among the religious people who were taunting Jesus. We're meant to see the shadow that lurks within each of us and the ease with which even the most devout and religious people can be swayed to treat others with cruelty and hate.

Second, we are meant to see the costliness of God's grace. Jesus' pain was not merely physical; it also was psychological and spiritual. The price of our redemption was profound, and the wounds by which we are healed cut deep. In this Jesus also models for us the way of love. We are meant to be willing to love sacrificially, and in so doing the world is changed. Others are moved by our sacrificial love, and we are changed by it; our faith and trust are deepened as we are willing to sacrifice for others.

Finally, we remember that the one to whom we pray in our darkest hour knew firsthand the feelings of hopelessness, doubt, and despair. Our King freely chose this path so that he might know what we experience in our times of pain. Jesus himself cried out to the heavens, "Why?" Yet as he made this cry, he was using words of a psalm that points toward God's ultimate deliverance.

We cannot end this chapter on the "cry of dereliction" without noting that this book will end as the season of Lent ends—at an empty tomb. In Matthew's Gospel, as well as in the longer ending of Mark's Gospel, these are not Jesus' final words. How tragic if these truly had been Jesus' final words. The feelings of abandonment and God-forsakenness, and even death itself, would not be the end of Jesus' story. Neither will suffering and death be God's final word for us.

———————

Forgive me, Lord, for the times I—like those who stood at your cross—have acted with cruelty. Thank you for identifying, by your suffering, with all who ever feel forsaken or cry out, "Why?" Help me to trust in you in my own times of adversity. Amen.

5.

"I Thirst"

> *After this, Jesus, knowing that all was now finished,*
> *said (to fulfill the Scripture), "I thirst." A jar full of sour wine*
> *stood there, so they put a sponge full of the sour wine on a hys-*
> *sop branch and held it to his mouth.*
>
> *(John 19:28-29 ESV)*

Nicodemus

I was drawn to Jesus since the first time I laid eyes on him. Three years later I stood by as he was crucified.

My name is Nicodemus, and the first time I heard Jesus speak was in Jerusalem. He preached with power and conviction, and his words were accompanied by the most remarkable deeds. The sick were healed, sinners came to God, and demons were cast out. He had a knack, however, for alienating my colleagues in the Sanhedrin. He healed on the sabbath, he did not follow our rituals and customs, and he had the irritating habit of pointing out our sins. Yet perhaps for these very reasons I was drawn to him.

I could not let my colleagues know of my interest in this radical preacher. When I finally met with him, I requested a meeting by night so that no one would see us together. It was at that meeting that he looked me in the eyes and said, "Nicodemus, you must be born again. You must be born not only of water but of the Spirit as well." What an utterly odd thing to say! But it was just like Jesus. I left him that night confused, feeling like I, a scholar and leader among our people, was a mere child in the eyes of this man. Once more I was deeply drawn to him.

The night before Jesus was crucified, the Sanhedrin had been called together for a hastily arranged meeting. My heart sank when Jesus was brought in by the Temple guard. I'm ashamed to say that I was silent as the others called for his death. I wanted to speak up for him, but I was too afraid. I knew I could lose everything if I spoke out against the High Priest and the others involved in this charade. Even now I'm embarrassed to tell you of my cowardice. That night he was sentenced to die, and I said nothing. I was so ashamed I dared not even look up at him as he stood there like a lamb before the butchers.

The next morning, as they led him to be crucified, I wanted to run and hide. Yet I knew that by my silence, I had allowed this to happen. I decided that at least I could have the courage to show up and see what my silence had wrought. I wanted him to see in my eyes my sorrow and pain and the deep regret I felt in not speaking out for him.

The women came to him just before he was crucified. They were given permission to offer him one last drink. The Romans did not know that the women, in compassion, had laced the cup of wine with poison meant to deaden the pain and to hasten his death. He tasted it, but noting its bitterness and understanding what they were doing, he refused to drink it. I turned away as he was nailed to the cross, and then I watched in silent agony as his cross was raised. I listened as my fellow priests hurled insults. Still I was silent. After some time the soldiers mocked him, offering him wine—a kind of toast to the crucified king—but they kept it just out of reach as he sought to drink.

Near the end of the ordeal, after he had hung there for six hours, he spoke again. He hadn't said a word in hours. He said, "I thirst." I could not stand it any more. At this point, watching him die, I found some small amount of courage. I no longer cared what anyone else thought. I took a branch, fastened a sponge to it, dipped it in wine, and lifted it to his lips. He drew from the sponge, and, shortly after, he breathed his last.

"I thirst." This simple statement that Jesus made before he died almost seems out of place among the other more dramatic statements he made from the cross. Yet this seemingly insignificant statement is recorded by John alone, and with John, almost every seemingly insignificant statement is a clue to the deeper meaning of Jesus' life, death, and resurrection.

Most interpreters of John recognize the deeper meanings within the words he recorded, but many disagree as to the meaning of this particular scene where Jesus states, "I thirst." In this chapter we'll explore the main lines of interpretation of this scene, and then we'll consider how the scene may speak to each of us on a personal level.

Before delving into the meaning of Jesus' words, "I thirst," let's consider the three different Gospel accounts of the offer of drink to Jesus at his crucifixion and what we're to make of each.

Three Offers of Wine

The First Offer

The first time that Jesus was offered wine occurred before he was crucified. Mark 15:22-23 says, "Then they brought Jesus to the place called Golgotha (which means the place of a skull). And they offered him wine mixed with myrrh; but he did not take it." Matthew, whose account of the Crucifixion is often word for word in agreement with Mark, includes this same statement but with a change in the last few words: "They offered him wine to drink, mixed with gall; but when he tasted it, he would not drink it" (27:34).

Scholars have had great debates over this story and what to make of it. Botanists, theologians, and biblical scholars have taken a stab at making sense of Matthew's use of "gall" and Mark's use of "myrhh" (15:23). Allow me to offer two possible interpretations.

A possible explanation is that the wine mixed with myrrh or gall was given routinely by the soldiers to further torment the victims of crucifixion. According to this interpretation, myrrh or gall was thought to make the victim terribly sick to the stomach, inducing vomiting. Imagine adding to the pain of crucifixion terrible stomach pain leading to vomiting from the cross. This is one possible meaning to the offer of wine mixed with myrrh or gall.

Another possible interpretation, and the one I think may be more likely as I've reflected upon this story and the commentary that has been written about it, is that myrrh and gall were ways of speaking of poisons that were thought to expedite death or possibly to deaden the pain. If this is the case, then someone showing compassion to Jesus was offering this drink. Because we know that most of the male disciples either had fled or were standing off at a distance and that women were standing near the cross, it is likely that this offer of wine was made by one or more women.

Yet notice that Jesus, upon tasting the wine mixed with gall, refused to drink it. In this case, Jesus stands in contrast to Socrates, who lived four hundred years before the time of Jesus. Socrates, when he was wrongfully sentenced to die, died a relatively speedy and painless death by drinking the cup of hemlock. It left him unable to feel pain, and ultimately he fell asleep and died. This story was well known around the world. Contrary to Socrates' example, Jesus was offered the poisoned drink but refused to take that which would deaden his pain and expedite his death. But if this was the reason for the offer of wine, why would he refuse such a drink?

Jesus was *intentionally* choosing to suffer. His suffering communicated both God's pain at the brokenness and sinfulness of the human race and the costliness of our redemption. As we learned in the previous chapter, his suffering also enabled him to identify with the suffering human beings face at times in our own lives. He would face the evil that humanity had to offer and the despair we sometimes feel without anesthesia. He would suffer for as long as it took for him to die. He faced sin, evil, despair, and death head on. This was

Jesus took the uncomfortable way, the inconvenient way, the way most of us don't want to go.

his mission. He did not wish to take the easier way out. He did it to fully identify with the suffering we experience as human beings and to show us the costliness of our sin and God's grace.

We live in a day when most of us tend to prefer the easy way out. If we feel bad, we want a pill. If things aren't going well, we want a quick fix, whether it has to do with our marriage or our physical body or our job. We like to take the comfortable way; we want to minimize pain and to avoid the way that's uncomfortable or inconvenient.

Jesus took the uncomfortable way, the inconvenient way, the way most of us don't want to go. In this he also invited us to take the difficult path at times in our own lives. That's what he meant when he said, "If any would be my disciples, they must deny themselves." (See Matthew 16:24.) Self-denial is something we're not very good at. But at times suffering or discomfort is redemptive.

When mission teams from our church went to help with cleanup after Hurricane Katrina, most of them went to Bay St. Louis, Mississippi. They could have found a hotel within a thirty-minute drive, enabling them to drive each day into the worst of the destruction zone to muck out the homes of the people staying there. But they didn't do that. Instead, each of these teams slept on the floor of the United Methodist Church. Some who went are used to staying in five-star hotels when they travel, but they chose to sleep on cots or sleeping bags on the floor and take showers in a trailer for a week. Why? Because they wanted to identify with the people of Bay St. Louis in their suffering. They freely chose discomfort for the sake of those they came to help. The discomfort was a part of the gift and part of the expression of the love of God through them. Jesus said, "If any want to become my followers, let them deny themselves and take up their cross and follow me" (Matthew 16:24). Sometimes Jesus calls us to take a more uncomfortable route, a more dangerous or risky route, so that the glory of God is revealed through our experience.

The Second Offer

The second offer of wine occurred sometime after Jesus was nailed to the cross. Luke records that the soldiers offered wine to Jesus in mockery, as though it were a toast. Luke writes, "The soldiers also mocked him, coming up and offering him sour wine, and saying, 'If you are the King of the Jews, save yourself!' " (Luke 23:36-37). In this case it is unlikely that Jesus actually would have been able to drink this wine. It likely was lifted up like a toast, just out of Jesus' reach, taunting him. In this I'm reminded of the way the soldiers mocked him by placing the crown of thorns on his brow, the reed scepter in his hand, and the cloak around his back as they taunted him, saying, "Hail, king of the Jews!"

The Third Offer

The third offer of wine is recorded in Matthew, Mark, and John, though John's account is somewhat different from the first two. Matthew and Mark write that just before Jesus' death, he cried out, "My God, my God, why have you forsaken me?" According to their accounts, it was in response to this cry that those near the cross took a stick, affixed a sponge to it, dipped the sponge in sour wine, and offered Jesus a drink. Sour wine was cheap wine, a wine that was commonly drunk by the poor and by the Roman soldiers. It also was known as wine vinegar; it had a bitter taste. Imagine drinking balsamic vinegar—not bad on a salad, but you wouldn't want to drink a cup of it. Yet if you were thirsty, even this bitter wine would be better than nothing.

In John's Gospel, the account is a little different. Let's consider again the words found at the beginning of this chapter:

> After this, Jesus, knowing that all things were now accomplished, that the Scripture might be fulfilled, said, "I thirst." Now a vessel full of sour wine was sitting there; and they filled a sponge with sour wine, put it on hyssop, and put it to His mouth. (John 19:28-29 NKJV)

To help us understand the passage, John explains parenthetically that Jesus spoke the words "I thirst" in order "that the Scripture might be fulfilled." What Scripture did Jesus fulfill by making this statement? Most scholars think it is Psalm 69:21b: "For my thirst they gave me vinegar to drink." When he said he was thirsty and was offered wine vinegar, Jesus was pointing us back to this verse from Psalm 69. He was saying, "Look, what I'm doing now was written centuries ago. It is part of God's plan that was set in place long before now."

Matthew and Mark tell us that "they" took a sponge, placed it on a stick, dipped it in wine vinegar, and gave him a drink. Then Jesus spoke his last.

There is yet a deeper meaning John is pointing us toward in his telling of this part of the story.

The Humanity of Jesus

Among several things interpreters of the Scripture see in this scene is a picture of the humanity of Jesus.

Nearly everyone who has been with a dying loved one knows that if the person is still conscious while approaching death, he or she becomes thirsty. Feeling extremely weak, a dying person will say, "I'm thirsty." Typically a nurse or hospice worker or loved one will bring a cup of ice chips and a spoon to place a chip or two on the person's tongue. Sometimes a cup of water and a straw is used. The person assisting puts the straw into the water, covers the end of the straw with a finger, capturing the water in the straw, and then places the straw in the dying person's mouth, carefully releasing the water by removing his or her finger. Sometimes the nurse or hospice worker will bring in a little sponge on a stick and soak it in water so that the dying person can draw water into his or her mouth through the sponge.

A similar kind of instrument was used with those who were dying on a cross in ancient times. The stick was much longer, but the approach was the same. The intent was to satisfy the thirst of the dying individual. This is the scene we see in John's Gospel.

Here's the point some think John was trying to make in his account of this scene: Jesus was fully human. Before his death, he thirsted as we thirst, and then he died as we die. This was an important point for John, because even as he wrote there were some Greeks who saw Jesus as a spirit who only appeared to be a man. Because such a spirit could not die, or even feel pain, he only seemed or appeared to die on the cross;

it was merely a drama. These Christians became known as *docetists* from the Greek word *dokeo*, which means "to seem."

Some of them went so far as to say that it wasn't really Jesus on the cross. They believed that when Simon of Cyrene carried the cross, he ended up taking the place of Jesus. The Son of God would never be defeated by evil people, nor would he suffer and die on a cross.

John wrote his Gospel at the time when some Greeks were suggesting these ideas, and it is possible that in recounting the thirst of Jesus he was saying essentially, "I stood by the cross. I saw him suffer. I heard him cry out, 'I thirst.' He did not merely seem to be suffering and dying. He was a man, dying there on the cross!"

Today there are still those who believe Jesus did not die on the cross, including most Muslims. Some Muslims believe that Jesus was crucified but was taken down before his death. Others believe that, while Jesus was crucified, God saved him from the cross, taking him into heaven before his death. Still others believe that another man was arrested and crucified in place of Jesus. Like the docetists, some Muslims say this was Simon of Cyrene; others say it was Judas Iscariot. In any case, most Muslims believe that Jesus was taken to heaven before death. Keep in mind that Mohammed composed the Quran five hundred years after John wrote his Gospel. John, on the other hand, claims to have been an eyewitness, drawing upon what he saw with his own eyes.

Jesus' words "I thirst" are one more example of Jesus' humanity. Clearly they are aimed to demonstrate that Jesus actually died on the cross. Jesus did not circumvent death any more than he circumvented the suffering he could have avoided by drinking the wine mixed with poison or painkiller offered to him before the Crucifixion. This is but one way of understanding the significance of Jesus' words "I thirst" recorded in John.

Jesus Finished the Cup

Another interpretation or meaning of these words, "I thirst," relates to an analogy Jesus used to describe his suffering. At the Last Supper, Jesus took the cup and said, "This is my blood of the new covenant" (Matthew 26:28 NKJV). Elsewhere Jesus is recorded as asking James and John, who wanted to sit at his right hand and his left hand, "Are you able to drink the cup that I am about to drink?" (Matthew 20:22). Likewise, in John 18:11, as Jesus was being arrested, Peter drew his sword; but Jesus told him, "Put your sword back into its sheath. Am I not to drink the cup that the Father has given me?" In each of these instances, Jesus used the metaphor of drinking as a way of describing the suffering he would "drink" as he suffered and died on the cross.

When we understand that on multiple occasions Jesus used the idea of drinking as a metaphor for the suffering he would endure, we see that Jesus' words "I thirst" may have pointed to something deeper. It is possible that Jesus' words were pointing toward his willingness to drink the cup of suffering and sin and hate—and to drink it down to the dregs. Or perhaps what he was pointing to was the fact that the cup was now nearly empty. His time of

It is possible that Jesus' words were pointing toward his willingness to drink the cup of suffering and sin and hate—and to drink it down to the dregs.

suffering was drawing to a close, and the cup of his suffering was now nearly empty.

This interpretation is consistent with John's statement: "After this, Jesus, knowing that all things were accomplished, . . . said, 'I thirst' " (John 19:28 NKJV). Jesus' thirst was an indicator that he had finished off the cup that his Father had given him; he had completed his mission to suffer and die on behalf of the human race. This is a second way of understanding the words of our Lord, "I thirst."

The Fountain of Living Water Dried Up

A clue to a third meaning of this statement of Jesus from the cross is found in Chapters 4 and 7 of John's Gospel. Let us look first at John 4—the only other time in John's Gospel when Jesus expresses that he is thirsty.

Near the beginning of Jesus' ministry, he came to the town of Sychar, which is modern-day Nablus. There he sat at Jacob's Well, while his disciples went into town. Soon a woman came to meet him. He asked for a drink, and she gave him one. Then he said to her, "If you knew who you were talking to, you would ask of me and I would give you living water and you would never thirst again" (see John 4:10).

The time of day when this conversation took place is significant. It was around noon. Usually women went to draw water in the morning and at night. They did not come mid-day. Yet this woman did. Why? Because she wanted to come when the other women would not be there to scorn her. This Samaritan woman had been divorced and remarried five times and was now living with a man who was not her husband. She did not have the social standing or security that came with marriage in ancient times. The other women in the community would have scorned her, seeing her as a sinner. For many years she had been thirsty for love, but none of her five husbands had satisfied this thirsting in her soul. She was thirsty for more than water on the day she arrived at Jacob's well.

Water is essential for life. We can live for weeks without eating but typically only three to five days without drinking. When Jesus uses this metaphor of thirst and living water in the fourth chapter of John's Gospel, he speaks of that which is essential for life.

I think of the "bore holes" our church is drilling in Malawi and how providing that clean, safe, life-giving water is a metaphor for the gospel we hope the people in the community will receive. We need both physical water and living water—spiritual water. This spiritual water is what our hearts yearn for; it is joy and hope, meaning and purpose, companionship and love, forgiveness and mercy. Jesus was saying to this woman, who had been trying her entire life to find something that would satisfy, that she had been looking in the wrong places. *He* was the source of this living water.

Likewise, in John 7, Jesus said to the multitudes in Jerusalem, "Let anyone who is thirsty come to me, and let the one who believes in me drink" (verse 37). And it is precisely with these two passages, John 4 and John 7, as a backdrop that John records that Jesus says, "I thirst." *What does it mean that the one who offers living water was now himself thirsty*? Can you feel the pathos in this scene and these words? The fount of living water is drying up. The source of life is dying. God enfleshed had come to earth to offer living water, and humanity had chosen to poison or destroy the Spring. Here on the cross the Spring is drying up; its water will cease to flow.

This scene also reminds me of Jeremiah 2:13: "My people have committed two evils: they have forsaken me, the fountain of living water, and dug out cisterns for themselves, cracked cisterns that can hold no water." The people had forsaken God and had chosen instead to drink the muddy run-off water, building cisterns to catch and drink it; yet even this could not satisfy.

As I reflect on Jesus' cry, "I thirst," I also am reminded of the words of Psalm 42:1-2: "As a deer longs for flowing streams, so my soul longs for you, O God. My soul thirsts for God, for the living God." Perhaps when Jesus said, "I thirst," he was speaking of his own inner thirst—his longing for God. Or perhaps Jesus was pointing back to his words from the Sermon on the Mount when he said, "Blessed are those who hunger and thirst for righteousness" (Matthew 5:6).

Jesus' words "I thirst" may have been intended for the people around him, or they may have been a prayer to God in which Jesus, like the psalmist and the prophet Jeremiah, thirsted for God. Perhaps his words were a prayer that recalled the words God spoke in Isaiah 41:17: "When the poor and needy seek water, and there is none, and their tongue is parched with thirst, I the LORD will answer them, I the God of Israel will not forsake them."

What are *you* thirsting for first and foremost in your life? What do you hope will satisfy you?

One day I was at a car show with a friend of mine, and we came to the top-of-the-line Corvette. It was a special edition. It had 750 horsepower and a price tag of $110,000. As I stood looking at that car, I thought, "That is so cool. Man, I'd like to have that." I told my friend jokingly, "Now that's the kind of car a pastor buys after retiring. You can't drive one of those as a pastor, but maybe when you retire."

We get hung up on things that we think will bring us satisfaction, but few of those things leave us feeling satisfied for long. Jesus' death on the cross for me and for you beckons us to thirst only for him.

That was a stupid thing to say. It would take half my retirement fund to buy that car. But let's say I actually saved over the next twenty years to buy that car when I retire. Do you think it would satisfy my thirst? Of course it wouldn't!

What about you? Would the next bigger house satisfy your thirst? Or how about a promotion? Or what if you were married to someone else? Do you think your thirst would be satisfied?

That's not the way it works. We get hung up on things that we think will bring us satisfaction, but few of those things leave us feeling satisfied for long. Jesus' death on the cross for me and for you beckons us to thirst only for him.

We've considered three possible ways of making sense of Jesus' words, "I thirst." Let's consider one more possible meaning we might find in this scene that is captured by a small detail only John includes in the telling of the offer of wine placed on a sponge and offered to Jesus.

The Hyssop Branch and a New Covenant

As we have already seen, Matthew and Mark tell us in their Gospels that someone fetched a stick, put a sponge on it, dipped it in wine, and raised it to Jesus. But John adds an interesting detail in his account. He indicates that the stick was actually a branch of hyssop. When John includes details such as this, he means them to be clues to help us interpret the story—to help us see the deeper meaning.

Hyssop is a small, bushy plant, and affixing a sponge of any size to a hyssop branch would be an odd and nearly impossible task. Perhaps John's point was not botany but theology.

It was Passover when Jesus was crucified. The Passover was when the Jews commemorated God's greatest act of salvation on their behalf—God's deliverance of his people from slavery in Egypt. On the last night of their slavery, God sent a terrible plague upon the Egyptians, one final act to force Pharaoh to release his people from bondage: the angel of death would pass through the land of Egypt, and every firstborn among the flocks and every firstborn child in every family would die. In preparation for this terrible plague and as God's provision to protect the firstborn of the Israelites, God told Moses to have the people slay a lamb. Before cooking and eating the lamb, they were to take the blood of the lamb and, *using a branch of hyssop*, to sprinkle it over their doorposts. When the angel of death passed through the land that night and saw the blood of the lamb upon the doorposts, it passed over those homes; the firstborn Israelite children were saved from death. That night, after the angel of death had passed through the land, Pharaoh relented, and the children of Israel were saved from slavery and oppression. After this they began their journey to the Promised Land.

Only John calls Jesus the "lamb of God." Only in John's Gospel does Jesus' crucifixion take place as the Passover lambs are being slaughtered in the Temple. For John, the hyssop branch was one more clue pointing to Jesus' identity as the sacrifice that would save the Israelites from death and deliver them from slavery to sin.

Likewise, in the Old Testament the hyssop branch was used in purification rites (see Leviticus 14:4-6, 49). When someone became unclean, after he or she had made a sacrifice, the priest would sprinkle the person with water—sometimes combined with ashes or blood from a sacrifice—and the person would be clean. The Book of Hebrews tells us that it was a hyssop branch that Moses used to sprinkle the scroll of the law and the people with blood as a way of initiating God's covenant with the people. As Moses did this, he said, "This is the blood of the covenant that God has ordained for you" (Hebrews 9:19-20).

You see, in telling us about the hyssop branch, John was not giving us a needless bit of information; he was pointing us toward the meaning of Jesus' death. Jesus was initiating a new covenant with God and humanity; he was cleansing all who would trust in him; he was saving us from slavery to sin; and he was delivering us from death.

Would You Offer Him a Drink?

As the people stood around the cross that day, watching Jesus die, someone in the crowd heard his cry, "I thirst," and had the courage to break away from the crowd, gather a branch of hyssop, affix to it a small part of a sponge, and lift it with compassion to Jesus' lips. It could have been the disciple John, or Jesus' mother. But as the chapter began, I imagined it being

Nicodemus, one of the priests and a member of the Council, who, as he watched Jesus dying, finally found the courage to be counted as a sympathizer with Jesus. Regardless of who it was, someone had the courage to risk the scorn of the crowd and to offer Jesus a drink before he died.

Today we still can offer him a drink. We do this when we see those who are physically or spiritually thirsty and we risk the scorn of others or simply go out of our way to offer them a drink. As Jesus said, "When you have done it for one of the least of these brothers and sisters of mine, you have done it for me" (Matthew 25:40 CEB).

Lord, be for me the source of Living Water. May my heart thirst after nothing as much as it thirsts after you. And may I, as one of your followers, extend water, both physical and spiritual, to all who are thirsty. Amen.

6.

"It Is Finished" . . . "Into Your Hands I Commit My Spirit"

When Jesus had received the wine, he said, "It is finished." (John 19:30a)

The curtain of the temple was torn in two. Jesus called out with a loud voice, "Father, into your hands I commit my spirit." When he had said this, he breathed his last. The centurion, seeing what had happened, praised God and said, "Surely this was a righteous man." (Luke 23:43-47 NIV)

The Centurion at the Cross

It was a job for angry men—men who had been abused as boys and those who were adept at compartmentalizing their work into the dark recesses of their mind when they came to the end of the day. We would brutalize men, drive spikes into their hands and feet, gamble for their final earthly possessions, and watch them die. Then we would go home and have supper with our wives and children.

It was about 8:30 in the morning when we led Jesus and the others to Calvary that day. I knew of Jesus. A friend stationed in Galilee told me how he had gone to Jesus and asked him to heal his servant. Jesus never even touched the servant; he merely spoke a word and the man was made well. My friend was convinced it was a miracle.

My friend told me that Jesus was not like the typical would-be messiahs. He wasn't raising up an army to drive us out of the country. He taught the people to love their enemies, to pray for those who harassed them, and to turn the other cheek when struck. I told my friend that we could use a few more like him in Judea! Yet here he was, being marched to "the Skull"—the place of crucifixion—after having been beaten and bloodied by my men.

As I looked at him—naked, the crown of thorns upon his brow—for the first time in a long time I felt a deep regret for what I was about to command my men to do. Yet this was my job, and he was just a Jew. Pushing back any semblance of compassion from the recesses of my mind, I gave the order for them to nail him to the "tree."

I watched him throughout the day, listening as he spoke. He took the abuse hurled at him with dignity and strength. It was as if he, with his crown of thorns, *really was* king and we were his rebellious subjects, whose rebellion would soon be put to an end. Yet far from calling for our destruction, this king pled for our mercy. Remarkable.

I watched as dark clouds rolled in at noon. An eerie feeling lingered for three hours. It was as if the heavens themselves were proclaiming the darkness of the deeds we were witnessing. Something felt dreadfully wrong. Then a small earthquake shook the ground. Some people fled in fear, terrified that this might be a sign from God.

At three o'clock Jesus cried out, "I thirst." One of the religious leaders surprised me by breaking away from his colleagues and giving Jesus a drink. Then Jesus said, "It is finished." What a strange thing to say as he approached his death. This was a cry of victory, a man successfully completing a mission. Just before he breathed his last he gathered his strength, pulled himself up by the nails in his wrists, and said in a loud voice, "Father, into your hands I commit my spirit." Then he bowed his head and gave up the ghost. It was the most remarkable death I'd ever seen, and I'd seen many. I stood there looking at this man, and I was overwhelmed by a sense of fear. What had we done? I turned to my men and said to them, "Surely this man was innocent. He was, as he claimed, the Son of God." And for the first time in years, I wept.

Jesus' last two statements from the cross were "It is finished," and "Into your hands I commit my spirit." In this chapter we will explore these final statements and the Gospel's record of what happened in the Temple in Jerusalem as Jesus was dying on the cross.[5]

"Finished!"

The Gospels of Matthew and Mark tell us that, as he breathed his last, Jesus cried out with a loud voice. Yet neither records what he said. John's Gospel tells us that what Jesus said was, "It is finished." Often we hear those words as Jesus' expression that his life was ebbing away: "It is finished." Some have heard this statement as a cry of defeat from a disillusioned prophet, as if Jesus were indicating that finally his suffering was over—something like the cry of a referee in a boxing match after he's given the ten count. But several things mitigate against this interpretation. Jesus told his disciples on multiple occasions that he was going to Jerusalem to die. His arrest, torture, and crucifixion were no surprise to him. He had come to Jerusalem for this purpose. This was not a cry of defeat.

Another clue that, when he spoke these words, Jesus did not mean he was defeated is found in the fact that he "shouted" these words. Actually, he shouted just one word in Aramaic, recorded in John's Gospel by one Greek word: "Finished!" or "Completed!" Will Willimon has described these words of Jesus as something similar to what Michelangelo might have said while looking up at the Sistine Chapel after he had completed the last brushstroke: "It is finished!" Something astounding, amazing, and awesome was finished as Jesus died on the cross—a masterpiece of love and redemption.

But what, exactly, was completed on the cross?

That's an important question, for it points to a much larger question: What purpose did Jesus' suffering and death serve? What did it accomplish? And how, exactly, did the death of Jesus accomplish these things?

Something astounding, amazing, and awesome was finished as Jesus died on the cross—a masterpiece of love and redemption.

When we talk about the significance of Jesus' death, we come to one of the most important doctrines of the Christian faith—and one of the most confusing: the doctrine of the atonement. The fact that you are reading this book that focuses on the final words of Jesus points to an interest in his death and its meaning. We've all heard that "Jesus died for you," but what does this mean? Jesus' death often is associated with the forgiveness of sins. Is his death only about forgiveness, or is there more? And regarding forgiveness, how does Jesus' death bring about our forgiveness and serve to make us "at one" with God? Or, to draw upon Jesus' final words in John's Gospel, what was "finished" when Jesus died?

I take great comfort in Leslie Weatherhead's comment in his classic book *A Plain Man Looks at the Cross*: "I cannot imagine any author, however great his scholarship or penetrating his spiritual insight, getting to the point where he felt he could so expound the message of the Cross as to leave no question unanswered and nothing unexplained."[6]

Both in college and in seminary I learned the historic "theories of the atonement" that have been used at different points in church history to explain the meaning of Jesus' death. I sought to explain each of these in my previous book *24 Hours That Changed the World* (Abingdon, 2009). The point I would invite you to consider here, and one that has been very helpful to me as I've wrestled to understand and explain the meaning of Jesus' death on the cross, is that Jesus was doing far more on the cross than any one theory or metaphor possibly can contain. Perhaps this is why neither the Gospel writers nor the apostles in their letters give us only one way to understand Jesus' death on the cross.

Jesus was doing far more on the cross than any one theory or metaphor possibly can contain.

John's Gospel is a great example. John begins his Gospel by calling Jesus "the Word made flesh." He seems to be saying that in Jesus, God has come to reveal God's nature and God's will to the human race. This should clue us in to the fact that Jesus' death is more like a sermon than a transaction.

A brief survey of John's Gospel reveals at least seven different ideas about the significance of Jesus' death.* He uses a host of metaphors, including at least five different Old Testament allusions that point toward differing meanings of Jesus' death. In John's Gospel, Jesus' death is an atoning sacrifice to save from sin; a substitutionary sacrifice to save from death; a demonstration of divine love for humanity; a model Christians are meant to look to in practicing sacrificial love; a compelling portrait of Jesus intended to stir the hearts of thousands more to come and follow him; a sign of God's ultimate triumph over death; and a dramatic reversal of the events of Eden following the disobedience of Adam and Eve.

The other Gospels add to these metaphors, though with far fewer than John. Paul uses several of the same metaphors that John uses in his epistles, but he adds to them. With so many metaphors that abound regarding the meaning of Jesus' death, it is unfortunate that many Christians seize only one theory of the Atonement and treat it as if that is all Jesus was seeking to accomplish on the cross.

Jesus is our Redeemer, our Savior, our High Priest, our Paschal and Atoning Lamb. He is our Liberator and the King who is willing to die for his people. Through his death he reveals our sinfulness, the costliness of grace, and the magnitude of God's mercy. On the cross he shows us what love looks

---

*See the Appendix.

like. In his death and resurrection he identifies with our pain, suffering, and human mortality; and in his resurrection he proves that he has overcome each of these. Jesus was doing all of this on the cross to redeem, save, and draw humanity to himself. This was the "it" that was finished as Jesus shouted his dying words.

The point of recounting this is, in part, to remind you that the language we use to describe what Jesus' death accomplished and what it means is metaphorical language meant to describe something so profound, so mysterious, so life-giving, and so life-changing that no one explanation or metaphor can do it justice.

I used to get stuck when I would think about the death of Jesus and exactly how it saves us. At some point I came to realize that the cross is not math or science; it is poetry lived out in human flesh. The cross is a divine drama in which God through Jesus is revealing the darkness of the human soul and the relentless grace and love of God for the human race. It is a sculpture that when seen from one angle is so horrible and repulsive you can hardly stand to look at it, but when viewed from another angle is so beautiful you cannot help falling to your knees in utter amazement. It is a masterpiece in which the Artist has painted at one and the same time a self-portrait revealing his character and a portrait of you—your need for mercy and his willingness to offer it to you. It is a love story that moves you to tears—one that begs to be read again and again.

John describes Jesus as "the Word made flesh." The cross is the climax of the story; John speaks of it as the moment of Jesus' glorification. He is glorified on the cross because the cross is the moment in which God gives himself, through his Son, to save us, God's creatures; the moment in which God convicts us of sin, reveals to us the costliness of grace, takes up the sins of the world, and shows us what love looks like so that we might follow in living lives of sacrificial love.

This is why we get stuck when we push any of the metaphors too far. Either they break down or we get confused. But when we move away from an overly literalistic reliance upon the metaphors and seek to understand that each is pointing toward spiritual and existential truths—love, redemption, grace, liberation—we begin to understand the power of the cross. In Jesus' death on the cross, God is speaking a profound message to us, and this message of the cross has the power to save us— our relationship with God and our relationships with others— and, in turn, to save the world.

When my children were living at home, the only way I knew how to tell them how much I love them was to say to them, "I love you so much that I would die for you without even thinking about it; I love you that much." I felt it, and I still feel it. That is what we see on the cross—the sacrificial love of God displayed. On the cross we see our brokenness and God's grace. We see our need to be loved and God's expression of love. We see a picture of how we're meant to live our lives from this time forward, and everything we see in the world around us we see in the light of the cross.

I love how the apostle Paul summarizes the gospel—the story of Jesus' life, death, and resurrection—and the work of the cross. He says, "It is the power of God for salvation to everyone who believes" (Romans 1:16 NASB).

The Temple Curtain Is Torn

As Matthew, Mark, and Luke seek to interpret and explain the significance of Jesus' death, they do so with an interesting detail. Luke tells us something happens just before Jesus breathes his last; Matthew and Mark say it happens just after he breathes his last. In any case, we discover from their accounts that the curtain in the Temple was torn in two. The fact that three of the four Gospels include this detail is significant. Let us take a closer look at the Temple curtain.

This diagram shows the inner court in the Temple in Jerusalem, which was perhaps a ten-minute walk from where Jesus was crucified.

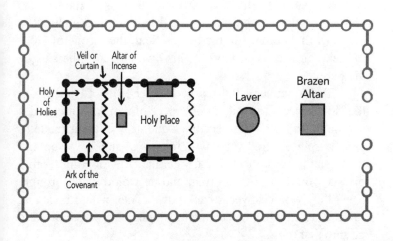

This inner court was the court of the priests. The priests would ascend up stairs to enter the Holy Place, where they would offer incense on the altar of incense. The Holy of Holies or the Most Holy Place was considered the throne room of God. In ancient times, the Ark of the Covenant was kept inside the Holy of Holies.

The Ark of the Covenant was a wooden box overlaid with gold that had two angels on either end, with their faces bowed and their wings meeting in the middle as if to form a seat or chair. This seat, called the Mercy Seat, was the throne of God. Inside the box were the Ten Commandments, a jar of manna—the food the Israelites ate in the wilderness—and the rod that God gave to Moses and Aaron that had budded.

Once a year the high priest would enter into the Holy of Holies to atone for his own sins and the sins of the people. First he would slaughter a bull and then a goat, sprinkling the blood of the animals on the Mercy Seat, the throne of God, to make amends with God for his own sins and the sins of the people.

The curtain or veil that separated the Holy of Holies from the Holy Place was made of one piece of woven fabric, and it is thought to have been very thick and heavy. It was made of blue, purple, and red yarns with images of angels woven into it. When the high priest would enter the Holy of Holies, other priests would raise the curtain and he would walk through. Then they would lower it back down. They would raise and lower it again when he came out. No one else was allowed to go into that room.

Matthew, Mark, and Luke tell us that when Jesus died, this thick curtain separating the Holy Place from the Holy of

Holies was torn in two. This was no small thing. It required a violent act of tearing.

Why did the Gospel writers think this was an important detail to include in their accounts of Jesus' death? The tearing of the Temple curtain is one more metaphor for what Jesus was accomplishing on the cross. Some have suggested that the tearing of the curtain was God's way of expressing his departure from the Temple. In other words, with the crucifixion of Jesus, God was turning away from God's people. With Jesus' death, the glory of the Lord had left the Temple. This is a powerful image of the grief of God at the death of God's Son. Most commentators see this tearing of the Temple curtain as a sign that at his death Jesus himself entered the Holy of Holies and made one final and perfect sacrifice to reconcile humanity to God. The curtain was not simply raised as it usually was on this occasion; it was torn in two—a powerful image that from this time on there no longer would be a need for the curtain. Through Jesus human beings would now come directly to God's Mercy Seat—to the cross to ask for mercy and to receive God's grace.

Jesus' Dying Prayer

After the Temple curtain was torn, Jesus offered one final statement. Once more, his dying words were a prayer.

We have noted that Jesus' first statement from the cross was a prayer. He prayed, "Father, forgive them; for they do not know what they are doing" (Luke 23:34). Then, around noon, he prayed from Psalm 22, "My God, my God, why have you forsaken me?" (Mark 15:34). I also have suggested that Jesus actually might have been praying to his Father when he said, "I am thirsty" (John 19:28).

Then, at the end, Jesus offered one final prayer: "Father, into your hands I commit my spirit" (Luke 23:46 NIV). These final words of Jesus are from another psalm—Psalm 31:5— which tells us that Jesus likely was reciting the psalm silently as he died. Here are the first five verses of the psalm:

> In you, O LORD, I seek refuge;
>   do not let me ever be put to shame;
>   in your righteousness deliver me.
> Incline your ear to me;
>   rescue me speedily.
> Be a rock of refuge for me,
>   a strong fortress to save me.
>
> You are indeed my rock and my fortress;
>   for your name's sake lead me and guide me,
> take me out of the net that is hidden for me,
>   for you are my refuge.
> Into your hand I commit my spirit. (Psalm 31:1-5)

This was Jesus' dying prayer. It was a prayer of absolute trust in God. Jesus had forgiven his enemies, offered mercy to a thief, prayed for his mother, come to a place where he felt abandoned by God, and expressed his physical thirst; but before his death, he declared the shout of triumph, "It is finished," and offered this beautiful prayer of absolute trust in his Father.

In his New Testament commentary on Luke's Gospel, William Barclay suggests that this prayer from Psalm 31:5,

"Into your hands I commit my spirit," was a prayer Jewish children were taught by their mothers to pray as they went to sleep each night. I find this a beautiful thought: that Mary may have taught this prayer to Jesus when he was a boy; and that Jesus, before he died, offered this simple prayer to his heavenly Father.

When we're facing darkness and despair, when we're facing the valley of the shadow of death, when we're facing the unknown, what should we pray? "Father, into your hands I commit my spirit."

On the cross, Jesus again was teaching us how to pray. When we're facing darkness and despair, when we're facing the valley of the shadow of death, when we're facing the unknown, what should we pray? "Father, into your hands I commit my spirit."

I recently was interviewed by a reporter preparing a story about the end of the world. She noted that the earthquakes, hurricanes, and revolutions in the Middle East, coupled with the end of the Mayan calendar, had increased the sense that people should be worried. She went on to describe Christians who were joining the chorus predicting that the end was near.

I told her that the signs of the end of the world found in Scripture have seemed applicable in every generation. Jesus was clear that no one knows the day or the hour that he will return and that the world, as we know it, will come to a close. The purpose of Jesus' words about his return are to encourage believers in the face of adversity and to invite his hearers to always be ready for the end. None of us knows when his or her life may come to an end, even if the world has not yet ended.

Those people who have died in earthquakes and tornadoes and hurricanes and tsunamis had no idea when they woke up that particular morning that it would be their last day. Nor did the approximately one hundred people who, according to statistics, will die today in car crashes across America, nor the three thousand people who will die today from a heart attack across the United States. Our aim is always to be ready.

What does it mean to be ready? In part, it means to have lived well, to have loved people, and to have faithfully served Christ every day. But in its most simple expression, it means to make Jesus' final words your own each day. It is to pray, with Jesus, "Father, into your hands I commit my spirit."

On a recent Sunday one of our members came to me to let me know that she was going to the Mayo Clinic for a serious surgical procedure. I knew she was anxious, and I invited her to meet me in our prayer chapel after worship so we could pray together. As we prayed together, I invited her to make Jesus' words her own each morning and each evening as she approached her surgery: "Lord, into your hands I commit my spirit."

I have encouraged our congregation to memorize this prayer and to pray it when they wake up and when they go to sleep. I've reminded them to pray it when they feel anxious or are facing uncertainty. I would encourage you to join Jesus in this prayer each day: "Father, into your hands I commit my spirit." When this is our daily prayer, we never have to be afraid. Jesus ended his suffering by teaching us how to live each day—not in fear but in confidence and hope: "Father, into your hands I commit my spirit."

Last Words to Live By

In these six chapters we have examined Jesus' final words from the cross. In the process, Jesus himself has taught us how to live and how to pray. We learned from him to pray for those who wrong us: "Father, forgive them; for they do not know what they are doing."

We saw that, even in his agony, Jesus was reaching out "to seek . . . and to save the lost" (Luke 19:10). We joined the thief on the cross in praying, "Jesus, remember me when you come into your kingdom" (Luke 23:42). And we heard his words of promise, not only for the thief but also for all sinners who call upon his name: "Today you will be with me in Paradise" (Luke 23:43).

We heard Jesus ask John to take care of his mother and his mother to take care of John, and in this we understood not only Christ's call for us to care for our parents and our children but also his call to care for those who are not our parents but who need our help.

We heard Jesus' anguish and his feelings of abandonment when he prayed, "My God, my God, why have you forsaken me?" In this we see that Jesus identifies with us in our dark nights of the soul. Yet Jesus, by virtue of this prayer, was also teaching us that in his darkest moment he was still praying and seeking God. Once more he models for us how we are to face the dark nights of our own souls.

In his cry "I thirst" (John 19:28 ESV), we saw the thirst of a real, dying man. But we also remembered the many images of thirsting and water that Jesus was pointing to in these words. They were not only a cry for drink for his parched lips, but also a call to his Father that his soul was thirsty and dry. In our spiritual thirst, we join him in this prayer.

We heard his shout of victory, "It is finished" (John 19:30a), as he completed the divine drama his Father had sent him to perform for us. Here, on the cross, was its climax, the moment when his glory was revealed as he laid down his life to save humanity. And we thank him for salvation that already has been attained for us.

Then, we heard the prayer his mother may have taught him as a little boy, a prayer of utter confidence and surrender to God, and we have made it our own: "Father, into your hands I commit my spirit" (Luke 23:46 NIV). This prayer from the cross enables us to live each day not in fear but in confidence and hope.

These are the final words of Jesus from the cross. These are words to live by. But though they were his final words before his death, there would yet be words after that.

Lord, thank you for the beauty, the majesty, and the wonder of the cross. Thank you that it was for me. In response may my daily prayer be, "Into your hands I commit my spirit." Yes, Lord, into your hands I commit my spirit. Amen.

Postscript:
The Words After That

Early on the first day of the week, while it was still dark, Mary Magdalene came to the tomb and saw that the stone had been removed from the tomb. (John 20:1)

After Jesus spoke his final word, he breathed his last. His body was removed from the cross, and with Pilate's permission he was buried. At last this man whose words had so angered and discomforted the religious leaders had been silenced.

But these words from the cross were not to be Jesus' final words. The powerful and joyous message of Easter is that there were "words after that."

In the Garden

Jesus' body was taken down from the cross and hastily buried in a borrowed tomb. The disciples went into hiding. The

Gospel accounts differ in some details regarding what happened next, but they all record that Mary Magdalene came to the tomb. She discovered the stone was rolled away from the entrance of the tomb and Jesus' body was missing.

No one was prepared for what occurred next. As Mary stood weeping at the tomb, a man she supposed was the gardener spoke to her: "Woman, why are you weeping? Whom are you looking for?" (John 20:15). Then the man spoke her name, "Mary!" and suddenly she knew that the gardener was Jesus.

The first words Jesus spoke after the final words he spoke from the cross were words of compassion to a woman who was weeping at his empty tomb. He spoke first to a woman—a woman out of whom, as Mark tells us in his Gospel, Jesus had cast seven demons. Today Mary's previous state would have been diagnosed as multiple personality disorder or schizophrenia or another psychological disorder. I mention this to say that Jesus not only healed this woman but also chose her to be the very first to receive the good news that he had been raised. Others may have seen her as a hopeless cause. Jesus did not. He had compassion on her, loved her, and honored her above all others.

The first words Jesus spoke after the final words he spoke from the cross were words of compassion. . . . In death and in his resurrected life, Jesus' first impulse was compassion.

In death and in his resurrected life, Jesus' first impulse was compassion. It was as he tenderly spoke her name that Mary finally recognized that the gardener was Jesus. It was this text that led C. Austin Miles in 1912 to pen the well-loved gospel hymn "In the Garden." You can hear Mary singing,

He speaks, and the sound of his voice is so sweet the birds
    hush their singing,
and the melody that he gave to me within my heart is
    ringing.
And he walks with me, and he talks with me, and he tells me
    I am his own;
and the joy we share as we tarry there, none other has ever
    known.[7]

The fact that John mentioned in his Gospel that Mary thought
Jesus was the gardener and that the place Jesus was buried was
a garden hints that there is much more than meets the eye in
John's telling of this story. John is pointing back to the Garden
of Eden (the opening words of his Gospel set the stage for this).
He is noting that Jesus, who here is the second Adam, has
opened the way through his death and resurrection for humanity to return to Eden. I explore this in greater detail in *24 Hours
That Changed the World* (Abingdon, 2009).

    Jesus' next words, according to Matthew's account, were
addressed to Mary and to "the other Mary" that Matthew
records was there: "Do not be afraid; go and tell my brothers
to go to Galilee; there they will see me" (Matthew 28:10).

    Jesus appeared first to the women. They courageously
had come to the tomb while the disciples were still hiding in
fear. There he called them to be the first to announce the good
news of his resurrection. I love this about Jesus. He took
those who were not allowed to be rabbis and preachers, one
of whom had been seen as "damaged goods," and chose them
to be the first to know that he was alive. Then he commis-
sioned them to share the good news of the Resurrection with
his disciples.

The women were to tell the disciples to go to Galilee where Jesus would appear to them. Galilee was a seven- to ten-day walk from Jerusalem. The women did as Jesus instructed them, but the men did not believe them.

On the Road to Emmaus

Perhaps because the disciples did not believe, or perhaps because Jesus himself could not wait seven days to see his friends, he began appearing to his disciples later that very day in Jerusalem. The first to see him were two followers of Jesus, a man named Cleopas and his unnamed friend. (As an interesting aside, Cleopas may have been the uncle of Jesus if he is identified with the Clopas of John 19:25 as many have suggested.) It happened this way . . .

> Now on that same day two of them were going to a village called Emmaus, about seven miles from Jerusalem, and talking with each other about all these things that had happened. While they were talking and discussing, Jesus himself came near and went with them, but their eyes were kept from recognizing him. (Luke 24:13-16)

Jesus had appeared as a gardener to Mary, and now as a stranger to two other disciples. He approached them, noting the sad expressions on their faces as they talked. In his translation of the New Testament, William Barclay translates this text by saying that "they stood with faces twisted with grief"[8] (Luke 24:17b). Let us focus on this story and the Easter lessons we learn from it.

We All Walk the Road to Emmaus Sometime

The two disciples' faces were "twisted with grief"—as undoubtedly were their hearts—as they walked the road to Emmaus. Each of us will one day walk our own road to Emmaus—a journey of grief, disappointment, and pain.

One day I received an e-mail from a friend whose twenty-three-year old son was celebrating his birthday that week in prison. She wrote of the sadness she felt for "the loss of our dreams for our son. The pain of seeing him imprisoned. The knowledge that he made so many mistakes and that we could not stop them." She was walking the road to Emmaus.

I received another note from a man who told me of his eighteen months of unemployment and his feelings of discouragement and disappointment. This was his road to Emmaus. You've surely walked this way yourself.

To these two disciples, their faces twisted in grief, Jesus came. Notice, however, that he came to them as a stranger. He came to these two as a fellow traveler and a stranger. I love what happened next. He did not immediately reveal himself to them. Instead, he slowly let them discover who he was. He asked them questions and then showed them from the Scriptures how the Messiah had to suffer and die.

When they finally arrived at Emmaus, the stranger bid them farewell and acted as though he were going on, still without revealing who he was. It was as if he were testing them to see if they remembered his teaching about welcoming the stranger. They had not forgotten, and they urged him to join them for a meal.

As they sat at supper with him, they asked him to offer grace; and there Jesus "took bread, blessed and broke it, and gave it to them. Then their eyes were opened, and they recognized him; and he vanished from their sight" (Luke 24:30-31). It was in hearing Jesus' words as he blessed the bread that they recognized him and knew that he had been raised to life.

Jesus Comes as a Stranger

The fact that Jesus came to these two disciples as a stranger is an important point.

I began writing this book in the weeks leading up to Easter. One afternoon during the week before Easter I stepped out of my office and noticed George and Vicki standing in the memorial garden located in a courtyard of our church. This was the one-year anniversary of their son Travis's death. Travis died in a car accident as he was driving back to college. His ashes are inurned in our memorial garden. I stopped to visit with George and Vicki, and they said, "Pastor Adam, you won't believe what happened this morning." They told me that when they woke up, they saw something on the front porch of their home. They opened the door and found that thirty-five of their friends and neighbors had bought dozens upon dozens of red geraniums and had left them there for George and Vicki to find on the morning of the anniversary of their son's death. There were notes of encouragement and a beautiful poem about God's care for their son and the promise that one day they would see him again.

Vicki said to me, "Adam, you have no idea what this meant to us. We felt God's love and the hope of the Resurrection through our friends and neighbors who remembered our son's death and showered us with love." Christ had come to George and Vicki on their Emmaus journey. While their faces were still

We experience Christ's presence through others.

twisted with grief, he came in the form of neighbors and friends and some who never left their names, saying, "We remember. We care. And your son is with God."

We experience Christ's presence through others.

Notice that these two disciples came to see who this stranger was only after they had offered him help. Had they not invited him in, they never would have seen the risen Christ. This points to another truth of the gospel: We experience the risen Christ when we serve others. Jesus noted that when we give food to the hungry or drink to the thirsty or clothing to the naked, or when we visit the sick and those in prison, it is as if we've done these things for him.

We have a ministry in the church I serve called "Beds for Every Body." The goal of this ministry is that no child in Kansas City will have to sleep on the floor because he or she does not have access to a bed. One of the places we deliver beds is to the inner-city schools our church partners with. Most of the children in these schools live below the poverty line. When a school gets word that a child doesn't have a bed, the administrators of the school call us. We deliver a bed to the child's home and set it up, including new sheets and pillows

and blankets. Before setting up the bed, our volunteers pray for God's blessings upon the child and his or her family. The volunteers regularly describe how they have felt Christ's

We meet the resurrected Christ when we serve strangers in need.

presence in the midst of these prayers and in the act of delivering children beds so they no longer have to sleep on the floor.

We meet the resurrected Christ when we serve strangers in need.

We Meet the Risen Christ in the Breaking of Bread

The last thing to note in Luke's Emmaus story is that it was in the familiar act of seeing Jesus break the bread and hearing him bless it that they finally recognized him. Luke wants us to see the Eucharist here. He's pointing us to the fact that we continue to see and experience the presence of the risen Christ in the blessing, breaking, and sharing of the bread of Holy Communion. He meets us at the Communion table as we eat and drink and kneel and pray. This meal is one of those "thin places," a term the Irish use to describe places "where the Presence is so strong that they serve as portals between this world and another."[9] The Celts were speaking of physical places. But anywhere the meal of bread and wine is shared in Christ's name has the potential to be one of those "thin places."

When I prepare for Holy Communion, I pause to fix in my mind the picture of Jesus sitting with his disciples, saying, "Do this in remembrance of me" (Luke 22:19). But I also picture him sitting with Cleopas and that unnamed disciple, breaking the bread and giving it to them, and then, in that moment, them recognizing him in the meal. After receiving the bread and wine, I kneel at the railing in the front of our church and talk with Jesus, saying something such as, "Lord, once more I need you. I offer my life to you. Fill me, forgive me, and heal me, I pray. And help me to love you and follow you." Like

Cleopas and the other disciple, I see my crucified and resurrected Savior in the breaking of the bread.

It is not only in Holy Communion but also more generally in worship that we experience the presence of Christ. There is something about gathering with others and praying, singing, listening, offering, and eating together that opens us to Jesus' presence.

We conduct a special service once a month at the church I serve for people with Alzheimer's, dementia, and memory loss. These are people who are a bit lost and disoriented on their journey to Emmaus. Several area nursing homes bus their residents over. Our staff and volunteers design the service with familiar old songs, prayers, and Scriptures. Recently we invited the children in the Kindermusic program—preschoolers who learn music in our church—to sing for the people in this service. Their anthem that day was the perennial children's favorite "Jesus Loves Me." As the children sang, the room full of senior adults with memory loss began breaking out in song, joining the children as they sang, "Yes, Jesus loves me! Yes, Jesus loves me! Yes, Jesus loves me! The Bible tells me so." For a moment these men and women, most of whom can no longer remember their names, remembered that Jesus the risen Christ loves them. This is the power of worship and Holy Communion.

After Jesus left, these two disciples noted how their hearts had burned within them as they had listened to the stranger talk. This is the power of his post-Resurrection words. When we listen as we are reading Scripture, hearing the sermon in church, or becoming quiet in the midst of prayer or Holy Communion, it is not uncommon for our hearts to burn within us as we hear him speaking to us.

These two ran back to Jerusalem, which was two hours away, and came to the hiding place of the disciples proclaiming that the women were right! Jesus was indeed alive!

"Peace Be With You"

Shortly after this, Jesus stepped from the shadows of the room and said, "Peace be with you" (Luke 24:36). This was not the first time Jesus had told his disciples not to be afraid or promised them peace. But he could tell they were terrified, and so, as John's Gospel tells us, he said a second time, "Peace be with you" (John 20:21).

This is precisely what the resurrected Jesus brings to us. We find in him our peace. I was speaking with several of the pastors who serve on staff with me about this text and one noted, "The resurrected Jesus didn't promise wealth or health or prosperity or power; what he promised was peace." As we trust in him—as we believe that he died and rose again—we don't find riches; we find peace and strength and courage so that we can face life with hope.

Listen carefully. The resurrection of Jesus didn't change the circumstances of those first disciples; it changed their perspective on their circumstances. It took those defeated and disillusioned disciples and gave them hope and joy and peace. That's what Easter still does for us today. Jesus' resurrection does not remove us from our present circumstances. But it does change how we see them. We face adversity, illness, and tragedy knowing that with God they will never have the final word. We believe that death has been defeated through Jesus' resurrection. This is what Paul captures in 1 Corinthians 15:54 when he writes, "Death has been swallowed up in victory."

Jesus' words continue to echo through history, coming to us in our moments of fear, in our times of adversity, and even as we walk through the valley of the shadow of death: "Peace be with you."

The Very Last Words

There is more that Jesus said and did over the next forty days before he ascended to heaven. It would take more than a postscript to unpack them all. But we dare not end this book of Jesus' final words without at least mentioning what Matthew tells us were really his final words before leaving this earth. Matthew describes it this way:

> And Jesus came and said to them, "All authority in heaven and on earth has been given to me. Go therefore and make disciples of all nations, baptizing them in the name of the Father and of the Son and of the Holy Spirit, and teaching them to obey everything that I have commanded you. And remember, I am with you always, to the end of the age."
> (28:18-20)

In his final words Jesus sent the disciples out to continue his mission to the world. The church has always understood that these words were not merely for those first disciples but for every generation since then. He was saying to them and to us, "I am sending you who follow me to go. Go and tell others the good news. Invite them to join you as my disciples. Baptize them. Teach them. Call them to obey the commands I have given you."

As we do these things, Jesus continues to speak. He speaks through us as we live and teach what he taught about the will of his Father. He speaks through us as we tell the story of his death and how, through it, he sought to redeem us, save us, heal us, and forgive us. He speaks through us as we tell the world the truth that neither hate nor evil nor even death could ultimately defeat him—or those who trust in him.

As we close this book, we come to the very last words that Jesus uttered before he left this earth. This is his very last sentence, and it is a promise—a promise that has the power to change how you live each day. He said to them, "Remember, I am with you always, to the end of the age" (Matthew 18:20).

––––––––––––

Lord, I do feel peace when I trust that you are with me always. I feel hope when I trust that you triumphed over the grave. Breathe on me your Holy Spirit, and grant me the power and courage to tell others of your love and to invite them to follow you. You are my crucified and risen Savior. Amen.

Appendix:
References to the Meaning of
Jesus' Death in John's Gospel

Lamb of God
John 1:29
The next day [John] saw Jesus coming toward him and declared, "Here is the Lamb of God who takes away the sin of the world!"

John 1:36
As [John] watched Jesus walk by, he exclaimed, "Look, here is the Lamb of God!"

When he called Jesus "the Lamb of God," John the Baptist was making a reference to multiple images of animal sacrifice in the Old Testament—from Abraham's sacrifice of a ram in place of his son Isaac (Genesis 22) to the Passover lambs slaughtered to save the Israelite children from death and deliver them from slavery (Exodus 12) to the various lambs slaughtered as burnt offerings for sin and guilt (see Leviticus). The image of animal sacrifice is clearly present, but the actual practice in the Old Testament would link Jesus to forgiveness, freedom from slavery and death, and an offering expressing gratitude.

Son of Man Lifted Up
John 3:14-16

"Just as Moses lifted up the serpent in the wilderness, so must the Son of Man be lifted up, that whoever believes in him may have eternal life. For God so loved the world that he gave his only Son, so that everyone who believes in him may not perish but may have eternal life."

Numbers 21 tells us that the Israelites sinned against God, and God sent poisonous snakes that bit and killed many people. But in mercy God commanded Moses to forge a bronze snake, mount it to a pole, and lift it into the air. As those who had been bitten by the snakes came to the bronze serpent and looked at it, they were delivered from the poison of the snakebite and lived. Presumably, looking upon the forged snake and trusting that this would accomplish what God promised brought about their healing and forgiveness.

Jesus' reference to Moses lifting up the bronze serpent in the wilderness seems to indicate that people would see him (Jesus) crucified and, by believing in him, would be delivered from death.

John 12:32

"And I, when I am lifted up from the earth, will draw all people to myself."

Here the image seems to be that of the martyr. By his death Jesus would draw many others to become his followers;

this is the power of martyrdom. One dies for a cause, and this willingness to do so draws others to the cause.

Grain of Wheat
John 12:24

"Very truly, I tell you, unless a grain of wheat falls into the earth and dies, it remains just a single grain; but if it dies, it bears much fruit."

Jesus—God's Son, the Messiah—dies as an expression of God's love and forgiveness and as a picture of "the way, and the truth, and the life" (John 14:6). Seeing Jesus, the Son of God, dying on the cross *for us* is deeply moving, and it draws us to him and to a willingness to follow him in demonstrating sacrificial love to others. This idea is captured in what sometimes is called the "subjective view of the Atonement."

New Covenant / Sacrificial Death
John 18:11

Jesus commanded Peter, "Put your sword away! Shall I not drink the cup the Father has given me?" (NIV).

After his last Passover supper with the disciples, Jesus took the cup and said, "This cup that is poured out for you is the new covenant in my blood" (Luke 22:20). In ancient times animals were sacrificed when two parties entered into a covenant. Jesus taught that by the shedding of his blood a new covenant was established between God and humanity. The cup he would drink was the shedding of his blood on the cross. Jesus' death is not only about forgiveness; he is the one sacrificed to make a new covenant between God and humanity.

John 15:13

"No one has greater love than this, to lay down one's life for one's friends."

Jesus spoke these words on the night he was arrested. Jesus' statement points to the idea of his death as the chief example of sacrificial love. On the cross he was proclaiming God's love for the world and showing his followers what it means to love one's neighbor.

John 19:13-14

When Pilate heard this, he brought Jesus out and sat down on the judge's seat at a place known as the Stone Pavement (which in Aramaic is Gabbatha). It was the day of Preparation of the Passover; it was about noon. (NIV)

When we come to the actual death of Jesus, John tells us that Jesus was crucified at the very time the lambs were being sacrificed for the Passover (the Synoptic Gospels—Matthew, Mark, and Luke—place Jesus' death the day after the Passover lambs were slaughtered). Once more John seems to want his readers to associate Jesus' death with God's deliverance of the Israelites from slavery and death, for the Passover lamb was slaughtered not for atonement but as a reminder of how God had delivered God's people.

Garden Metaphor
John 19:41-42

At the place where Jesus was crucified, there was a garden, and in the garden a new tomb, in which no one had ever been laid. Because it was the Jewish day of Preparation and since the tomb was nearby, they laid Jesus there.

John 20:15

[Jesus] asked her, "Woman, why are you crying? Who is it you are looking for?" Thinking he was the gardener, she said, "Sir, if you have carried him away, tell me where you have put him, and I will get him." (NIV)

Jesus was crucified near a garden, was buried in a garden, and was raised from the dead in a garden. Moreover, when he first appeared to Mary on Easter morning, he appeared as a gardener. All of this is likely John's way of pointing back to the garden of Eden. John's Gospel began with the words "In the beginning," a clue as to what was to come in the Gospel. If this is the case, Jesus' death and resurrection brought about the reversal of what happened in Eden—the reverse of the curse that came from human disobedience to God. Jesus was restoring paradise.

Notes

1. Paul Tillich, *The New Being: Existential Sermons* (Scribner's, 1955), p. 7; found at: http://www.scribd.com/doc/6410214/Paul-Tillich-The-New-Being-Existential-Sermons-1955) (accessed 8/27/2011).

2. The 2011 Retirement Confidence Survey, March 2011, Employee Benefit Research Institute, © 2011, cited in Charles Schwab's "Baby Boomer Reality Check," April 13, 2011, http://www.schwab.com/public/schwab/resource_center/expert_insight/retirement_strategies/planning/baby_boomer_reality_check.html (accessed 9/20/11).

3. Fleming Rutledge, *The Seven Last Words From the Cross* (Kindle Locations 202-204), Kindle Edition, 2011.

4. Aleksandr Isaevich Solzhenitsyn, *The Gulag Archipelago 1918–1956: An Experiment in Literary Investigation*, translated by Thomas P. Whitney and H. T. Willetts (Harper & Row, 1997), p. 168.

5. I have combined the final two statements of Jesus for two reasons: This book is meant to coincide with the six weeks of Lent, hence six chapters are required. Also, each statement is claimed to be the final words of Jesus from the cross. At the same time, each statement easily merits its own chapter, and if a pastor were preaching from either of them, each would merit its own sermon.

6. Leslie Weatherhead, *A Plain Man Looks at the Cross* (Nashville: Abingdon Press, 1945), p. 21.

7. C. Austin Miles, "In the Garden," *The United Methodist Hymnal* (Nashville: The United Methodist Publishing House, 1989), 314.

8. *The Gospel of Luke, New Daily Study Bible* (Louisville: Westminster John Knox Press, 1975, 2001), p. 348.

9. Barbara Brown Taylor, *Leaving Church: A Memoir of Faith* (New York: Harper Collins, 2006), p. 80.

The Journey

Journey with Adam Hamilton on the page and on video as he travels from Nazareth to Bethlehem in this unique new look at the birth of Jesus Christ.

Hamilton once again approaches a world-changing event with thoughtfulness and wisdom, just as he did with Jesus' crucifixion in *24 Hours That Changed the World*.

Using historical information, archaeological data, video excursions in the Holy Land, and a personal look at some of the stories surrounding the birth, the most amazing moment in history becomes more real and heartfelt as readers walk along that same road.

DVD with Leader Guide
Join Hamilton in the Holy Land by video, exploring many of the locations where the Christmas story took place. Includes a Leader Guide.

The Journey: A Season of Reflections
Four weeks of devotions ideal for individual use or as a companion to the primary book during Advent.

Youth Study Edition
Everything needed to conduct a 5-week study for ages 13-18. Use with the adult-level DVD.

Children's Study Edition
Everything needed to conduct a 5-week study for ages 3-12. Includes reproducible handouts.

On the Way to Bethlehem
An accompanying children's book.

⑂ Abingdon Press

Coming soon from Adam Hamilton

Adam Hamilton has visited the Holy Land to explore the birth of Jesus in *The Journey* and his death and resurrection in *24 Hours*. Now, join him as he follows in the footsteps of Jesus from the baptism and temptations and moving through his ministry: the people he loved, the healing he brought, the parables he taught and the enemies he made.

A new book and video study coming December 2012.

24 Hours That Changed the World

ADAM HAMILTON

Walk with Jesus on his final day.

Sit beside him at the Last Supper.

Pray with him in Gethsemane.

Follow him to the cross.

Desert him. Deny him.

Experience the Resurrection.

No single event in human history has received more attention than the suffering and crucifixion of Jesus of Nazareth. In this heartbreaking, inspiring book, Adam Hamilton guides us, step by step, through the last 24 hours of Jesus' life.

"Adam Hamilton combines biblical story, historical detail, theological analysis, spiritual insight, and pastoral warmth to retell the narrative of Jesus' last and greatest hours."

—LEITH ANDERSON,

author of *The Jesus Revolution*

ISBN: 978-0-687-46555-2

Devotions and Study Resources

For the Lent and Easter season, Adam Hamilton offers 40 days of devotions enabling us to pause, reflect, dig deeper, and emerge changed forever.

ISBN: 978-1-426-70031-6

Travel with Adam through this companion DVD visiting the sites, walking where Jesus walked along the road that led to the pain and triumph of the cross.

The DVD includes seven sessions plus an introduction and bonus clips. Each session averages ten minutes each.

ISBN: 978-0-687-65970-8

Also available:

Older and Younger Children's study sessions and youth small group resources.

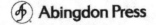

Abingdon Press

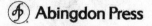

ENOUGH

With more than 120,000 copies sold since its initial 2009 release, *Enough* has changed countless lives by offering hope, spiritual direction, and assurance that anyone can, with God's help, find their way to a place of financial peace and contentment.

In this new and expanded hardback edition, Adam Hamilton shows there is a way back to a firm spiritual and financial foundation. In these pages, readers can find the keys to experiencing contentment, overcoming fear, and discovering joy through simplicity and generosity.

This book will change your life by changing your relationship with money.

ISBN: 978-1-426-74207-1

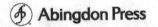

AVAILABLE WHEREVER FINE BOOKS ARE SOLD.

For more information about Adam Hamilton, visit www.AdamHamilton.AbingdonPress.com